Parenting
in an
Unresponsive
Society

Parenting in an Unresponsive Society

Managing Work and Family Life

Sheila B. Kamerman

THE FREE PRESS
A Division of Macmillan Publishing Co., Inc.
NEW YORK

Collier Macmillan Publishers
LONDON

The Free Press
A Division of Macmillan Publishing Co., Inc.
866 Third Avenue, New York, N. Y. 10022

Collier Macmillan Canada, Ltd.

Library of Congress Catalog Card Number: 80–641

Printed in the United States of America

printing number

1 2 3 4 5 6 7 8 9 10

Library of Congress Cataloging in Publication Data

Kamerman, Sheila B
    Parenting in an unresponsive society.

    Bibliography: p.
    Includes index.
    1. Children of working mothers—United States.
2. Parenting—United States. 3. Sex role. I. Title.
HQ777.6.K35   306.8'7   80-641
ISBN 0-02-916730-2

For Mort

Contents

Acknowledgments

THE CONCLUSIONS of this report are the author's, and do not reflect the opinions of either the sponsoring agency, the administrative auspice, the project staff or the interviewees. Nevertheless, the study could not have been completed without the cooperation of all the above. I am particularly grateful to:

Joanne Hansen, who as research associate on the project, did much of the interviewing, coordinated and supervised project staff interviewers, and contributed generally to much of the project work.

The project staff interviewers (Nancy Fowlkes, Betty Graham, Anna Morton, Joan Rosado, Barbara Spencer, Marcia Wylie) who helped to recruit our sample as well as to carry out the interviews in ways that assured us rich data for our report.

The County officials and agency directors and staff who also helped recruit interviewees for us, and cooperated in a variety of other ways to facilitate completion of the study.

Alfred J. Kahn, my colleague, who read an earlier draft of this report, and whose advice and criticism throughout the progress of this study added immeasurably to whatever clarity and coherence this final report may possess.

Edith Grotberg, Director, Research and Evaluation Division, Administration for Children, Youth and Families, (ACYF) DHEW, the Project Officer for the study, who provided support and encouragement for the project, from its inception.

Most of all, however, I want to thank the 205 "Working Mothers" who participated in the study. Their stories are what made the study worthwhile—and the report possible. In this report and in my subsequent work, I would hope somehow to make others more sensitive to the needs and problems of working mothers with young children and the Herculean efforts these women make to fulfill their central and interrelated roles in work and family life.

Sheila B. Kamerman
Director
Working Mothers Research Project

Parenting in an Unresponsive Society

Women in America Today: Trends and Developments

Lifestyles and Patterns

JOAN L.: SUPERWOMAN

"When we first talked six months ago, I was so sure of myself," Joan said. "Wife, mother, career person—I was a superwoman and I had no doubts about my capacity to manage. With a six-month-old baby, I was already back at work three months since the end of my maternity leave, commuting nearly two hours daily to hold a vice-presidency in one of the city banks.

"When my husband and I got married four years ago, we were both twenty-eight. Our careers and our life-styles were already established. We were a typical young couple on the way up and we planned accordingly: one last trip to Europe to be followed by a house in the suburbs the next year and a child—an only child—the year after. We would both continue to work, of course. Our salaries were almost the same and we couldn't possibly support our life-style with only half the income.

"Everything went according to plan except this superwoman isn't so super any more and I'm not exactly sure what's wrong.

"The first months after David was born were traumatic. No matter what I thought before, no amount of reading or talking to people can prepare a woman for the experience of a first child. Books helped prepare me for childbirth, nursing, minor illnesses, and how to play with the baby. But nothing prepared me for the totality of the experience itself or for having to integrate it into an already complicated life.

"I was fortunate in finding a motherly babysitter who would take care of David during the day when I returned to work. I'm very well organized and I soon developed a regular routine and thought everything was under control. I get up at 6 A.M., give the baby a bottle and play with him, shower, dress, fix breakfast for my husband. At 7:45 I drive to pick up the sitter and bring her to the house. We talk about the day's program and then I leave for work. In the evening, everything is reversed. I return home, take the sitter home, play with the baby, start our dinner, bag the next day's lunches, feed the baby, and sit down—exhausted—to have dinner with my husband. He does the dishes afterwards while I put the baby to sleep. Weekends involve marketing, laundry not done by the sitter, playing with David—but still not enough sleep.

"By now, six months later, what I'm most conscious of is being constantly tired. I knew I would have to give up all volunteer and social activities once the baby came, but I hadn't anticipated the total lack of free time, the constant real or imagined pressures at work and at home and the tight schedule which governs all my waking hours.

"Before David was born, my husband and I had agreed we would share responsibilities, but somehow this seems to mean he plays with the baby while I cook or he does the dishes, but not very much more. All the real responsibility is on me. My working hours are coordinated with the sitter's while my husband comes and goes as he chooses. Meal planning and preparation is a constant chore: three meals daily for us, three different ones for the baby, lunches and snacks for the sitter. If we run out of milk in the middle of the week, it's my fault. And the biggest fear of all is that the sitter may get sick. The one time that happened I was the one who had to figure out how to cover and ended up staying home myself.

"So here we are. We both have great jobs, a beautiful house in the town with the best public school system in the state. We stretched what we could really afford now in order to buy this house so that David would have a good school when he's ready. Our salaries are high and probably will get higher, so we can manage the house and in-home child care, too. David is really a good baby and a joy to play with and take care of and we were lucky to find a very warm, relaxed woman who is wonderful with him. We have what everyone would consider to be the ideal arrangement.

"With it all I seem to be overwhelmed and exhausted. It seems to me that Jim, my husband, should be helping more. Doesn't being a parent include fathers as well as mothers? How do people manage who have no husbands? How do they manage when they have two children?"

ANN M.: SHARING PARTNERS

Ann is a licensed practical nurse who continued working after her child (now eight months old) was born, except for the unpaid three-month maternity leave (with job protection and fringe benefits maintained) provided by the hospital where she works. Her husband is a policeman. Ann wished she could have remained home at least until her son was six months old, but the family needed her income just to manage basic expenses. Both she and her husband work different shifts covering different times of the day as well as different days of the week, and their routines change from month to month. Ann deliberately selected shift work, even knowing that her husband's job required it, too, so that at least part of the time each parent could carry major child-care responsibility. Her basic work day is 7:30 A.M. to 3:30 P.M. On the days her husband is working at that time, she gets up at 5:00 A.M. in order to bring Timothy to the woman who cares for him during the day when both parents are working. Ann changes the baby, gives him his bottle, plays with him, and then on her way to work drops him off at the home of a woman who takes care of him and one other child. On those days, her husband picks up the baby when he gets off duty and cares for him until she returns home. Her husband works progressive, rotating shifts so each week his hours are different. They take different days off even though it limits their time together, so that four out of seven days one or the other parent cares for Timmy and only three days a week is he cared for by somebody else.

Because of the pressures on both parents, housework and meal preparation are deliberately casual. Often when both of them are home they take the baby and go out to McDonald's and eat there. All recreational activities include Timmy. They take him with them to visit friends or family and have eliminated anything else, such as a movie, where they couldn't bring the baby.

Everything they do is discussed jointly and shared; the center of attention is the baby, and their daily lives are planned around his needs. They even planned to take separate vacations in order to maximize the amount of time that each can devote to the baby. And the plans are long-term. Ann says that they have decided that when Timmy is four, he should be entered into nursery school, and at that point she will have a second child.

JUDY S.: GOING IT ALONE

Judy is a secretary in an office twenty minutes away from the apartment house where she lives. She was just notified by the director of the day care center that next month, in September, there will be a place for her eighteen-month-old Susie if she wishes. With some trepidation, Judy has decided to place the baby there. She used to bring her daughter to her mother's, but it will be too much for her mother this coming year because it would mean having two preschoolers at once. Last year, Jimmy, her son who is five now, was in the day care center and loved it. This year he will be entering kindergarten at the local school, but it's only half a day. Judy's neighbor, who has an older child at the same school, will bring Jimmy to school in the morning. Her mother, who lives nearby, will pick him up and take him to her house for the afternoon. But now that she will have Jimmy from noon until 5:30, she feels it is too much for her to manage the younger one, too. And it is too expensive for Judy to have the two in day care, even though she does not pay the full fee.

Judy's husband left her last year. Although he is supposed to contribute child support, he moved six months ago and she has not heard from him since. She went back to work when he left, and fortunately she had no trouble getting a job even though her $10,000 a year salary is not enough to manage on. She copes by doing free-lance typing at home, on weekends and evenings, but it means she works six days a week and often until midnight.

Her new routine involves an 8:30-to-4:30 work day. She gets up at 6:00 A.M., gets the children up, dresses the baby, prepares breakfast for the three of them, straightens up the two-bedroom apartment while Jimmy dresses himself. Jimmy goes down the hall to the neighbor's, and Judy takes the baby to the day care center on her way to work. After work she picks up the baby, collects Jimmy from her mother, who has already given him supper, and then goes home. She plays with the children for a while, feeds the baby, bathes them both and gets them ready for bed. She thinks it is very important that she give them extra attention since they have a father who has no interest in seeing them. Most nights she types from the time Jimmy goes to bed until midnight.

The weekends are the only time the apartment gets any real attention, according to her. One day each weekend is devoted to household routines: She cleans the house, does the laundry, and takes the children with her when she markets. The other weekend day she types. Her neighbor down the hall in the building exchanges babysitting arrangements with her sometimes so Judy can do something special with Jimmy and leave the baby. Once in a long while she might go to a movie with one of the other women in her office. The last such occasion was two months ago.

How typical are these stories? How do other women in similar circumstances manage? Do the experiences of these women mean anything for how America's young families are living today? Can we learn anything from their efforts at managing complex and demanding lives?

The Study

What follows is the report of a study of working mothers with very young children: how they manage their daily work and family lives; what they identify as their major needs and problems; how they cope with meeting these needs or resolving these problems; what in their view are the consequences of their "solutions" for family life, children, their work, and themselves as individuals as well as parents.

The study was not designed to survey a precisely representative sample of such women, but rather to explore in some depth a group of black and white women, from different types of families and different socio-economic levels, at the point of a major life transition for women in work and family life. All these women are either reentering the labor force after a brief time out for childbearing and child care or continuing work despite a new baby. Neither the women themselves nor the communities in which they live can be described as truly typical or representative of the whole United States. In some respects their lives are easier than other women's in similar circumstances in that they live in a relatively affluent suburban community with fairly extensive facilities. On the other hand, because it is a suburban area where public transportation and child-care services are not as readily available as they are in some large cities, there are problems in managing work and family responsibilities.

However, although these women are not fully representative of other working mothers in America, their experiences are certainly not unique. Living in a suburban area is increasingly characteristic of a large part of the population in this country. The suburbs have grown at a faster rate than either central city or nonmetropolitan areas, and within less than a decade about half of the population is expected to live in suburbia. Moreover, and most important, these women are undergoing what is increasingly becoming the modal experience for adult women in the United States. They are in the labor force, and they are parents.

The ultimate goal of this study is to expand knowledge about family functioning and the interrelationship between families and the social institutions they deal with, in order to contribute to the ongoing debate regarding public policy and social provision. The immediate objective, however, is to develop useful insights into the kinds of problems that exist as a consequence of the working mother role, and the approaches which women use in solving their problems—in particular, with the roles played by both formal and informal family support systems.[1] Thus, we pay particular attention in this study to (a) how women manage the central tasks of child care, housekeeping, and housework; (b) how tasks and decisions are shared with spouses (when and if they are present); (c) how women feel about work, family, and combining the two; and (d) what they view as problems and how they solve them.

Why the Study?

However poignant the personal stories that open this report may be, a question remains as to what is the significance of the subject for serious study?

The "family" has clearly emerged anew in the late 1970s as a central subject for discussion, debate, research and writing in both scholarly and popular arenas. Anxiety over whether or not the family as a basic social institution is dying has diminished. In its stead has emerged a fairly broad consensus around the position that the family is "here to stay," but that it certainly is changing.[2]

Although not unique to this decade, two developments became especially visible and significant as the rate of change accelerated sharply during the 1970s: the first and most important, if only because it already characterizes more than half the adult women in the United States, is the entry of women into the labor force. This development has been described repeatedly in words used by the economist Eli Ginzberg as "the single most outstand-ing phenomenon of the twentieth century," with implications for every aspect of our daily lives. The second is the growth in fe-male-headed families, now constituting more than 14 percent of the families in the United States. This latter phenomenon is of in-creasing importance because, among other things, it is now esti-mated that close to half the children born since the middle of the 1970s (46 percent) will experience living in a one-parent family at some point as they grow up. Moreover, if more than half the women with children now work in the United States, living in a one-parent family makes it even more likely that a child will have a working mother.

Clearly, *for a child born in the last quarter of the twentieth century in the United States, as in other industrialized societies, being reared and cared for in a family in which both parents—or the sole parent—works, will be the normal experience.* Given the fact that in industrialized societies such as ours the work place and home are physically separate, how parents cope with parent-ing and employment roles becomes increasingly important to the society as a whole, as well as to individual families and family members attempting to manage this complex role.

Women, Children, and Families in the United States Today[3]

WOMEN IN THE LABOR FORCE

Women are in the labor force. Despite the recent increase in unemployment rates, women continue to enter the labor force, and the likelihood is they will remain there and that more will enter.

It is not that women have never before been workers. Any reading of social history from the sixteenth to the eighteenth cen-tury shows otherwise. But in the past women worked—as men did—in nonmonetized work at or near home, in farming or

(later) in home-based cottage industry. Only with industrializa-
tion did home and work place become separated. And only for a
brief time in history, from the mid-ninteenth to the mid-twentieth century, was there a small stratum of middle-class and (later)
working-class women who remained at home, working neither
on the farm in domestic industry nor in the factory, fully at
leisure apart from child care and housework, and often even having assistants in these tasks, too. In short, the "modal" family,
with the father at work outside the home supporting the mother
as a full-time homemaker and child-care person (and consumer
of cultural advantages), is a relatively recent phenomenon growing out of particular economic and social circumstances in modern society. The pattern spread briefly, to many other groups
and, in part, explains the policy which underlies the Aid to Families with Dependent Children (AFDC) program. Since World
War II, it has begun to break up once again.

Since 1950 the participation rate of women in the labor force
has increased from about one-third to almost one-half (48 percent in 1977). At the same time, primarily as a result of earlier
retirement, the participation rate of men in the labor force has
decreased from 86 to 78 percent. Participation rates for men between the ages of twenty-five and fifty-four, the peak years of
family responsibilities, are a little above 90 percent. Among
women, 67 percent of those in their early twenties and close to 60
percent of those aged twenty-five to fifty-four are in the labor
force. This trend is expected to continue, with still more women
entering the labor force during the next decade, and a projected
participation rate in 1990 of close to 70 percent of those aged
twenty-five to fifty-four.

Since World War II, the trend in labor force participation of
women has been clear-cut, representing a particularly significant
pattern for those interested in the problems of how parents are to
cope both with family and work responsibilities. The first cohort
to expand its participation rate consisted of those women aged
forty-five to fifty-nine who had largely completed their childrearing responsibilities. Since the mid-1960s, however, the greatest labor force increases have occurred among women under age

forty-five, especially married women living with their husbands. Thus, the proportion of married women in the labor force with school-age children nearly doubled between 1950 and 1976, and the participation rate of wives with preschool children tripled. Moreover, *the proportion of mothers participating in the labor force grew at a faster rate than for all other women*. By 1977, more than half the mothers of children under eighteen (51.7 percent) were in the labor force, as against 48 percent of women generally.

Since 1970 the greatest labor force increases have occurred among married women under age thirty-five with children under three. Furthermore the long-term pattern in which large numbers of women withdraw from the labor force in their twenties to rear children has apparently ended. Not only were close to 60 percent of the twenty- to twenty-four-year-olds in the labor force in 1970 and 67 percent in 1977; but for the first time there has been no significant decline in labor force participation for women aged twenty-five to twenty-nine, the prime childbearing years. This suggests both increased commitment of women to permanent labor force attachment and work behavior on their part increasingly similar to that of men.

Finally, two more related developments may be predictive:

1. Among women aged twenty-five to fifty-four the effect of higher education on labor force participation is particularly pronounced, with the labor force participation rate for women college graduates being over 70 percent. Given the rapid and steady increase in women's educational attainments since 1950, there is great likelihood of higher overall rates for women.

2. Women with one or two children tend to work more than those with three or more. The long-term trend to have fewer children should contribute still further to this growth of the female component in the labor force.

In short, women are working in growing numbers, and there is progressively less difference between the labor market behavior of mothers and those of all women, and between women and men. Moreover, responses to national surveys regarding women's attitudes toward work indicate that they, like men, view work as central to their identities.

Furthermore, women work for the same reason men work: they need the money. Of the 38 million women in the labor force in 1976, 9 million were single; more than 7 million were widowed, divorced, or separated; and nearly 10 million were married to husbands earning less than $10,500 per year or less than what was regarded as needed to meet the minimum requirements of a family of four as defined by the Bureau of Labor Statistics. Thus, for 26 million women—seven out of ten working women—employment is a compelling economic necessity. For many of the others, their earnings contribute significantly to household and family income, often providing the margin that makes for a comfortable, decent standard of living.[4]

The society has changed, and the two-earner family has emerged as the dominant family type. Less than 16 percent of all families match the image of a traditional family with a husband who is the sole breadwinner and a wife who is a full-time, at-home housewife. Nearly half of all families include an employed woman. Among husband–wife families, less than one-third of all husbands are the sole breadwinners. About 10 percent of all employed wives are the sole wage earners in their families, and another 12 percent earn more than their husbands.

This growth in the employment of married women with children has important consequences for family life-styles. Women often have to shoulder the triple burden of a job, housework, and child care, creating fatigue, resentment, and family stress. Alternatively, husbands or other family members—or services purchased from the market outside the family—must contribute in order to alleviate the burden.

Furthermore, the financial support system of families changes when there are two earners. Inflation, taxation, and aspirations for a higher standard of living have made families increasingly dependent on the earnings of two individuals. In 1976 median family income for all husband–wife families was $16,200. For husband–wife families with wives in the paid labor force, the median income was $18,830, or 35 percent higher than the median income ($13,930) for husband–wife families in which the wives were not in the paid labor force. Married women who work full time contribute 39 percent of family income.[5]

WOMEN ALONE

For women rearing children alone, without the help of husband and father, the burden is even heavier. Here, too, the experience is becoming increasingly common for a large proportion of the population. Although 84 percent of all families were husband–wife families in 1977, 14 percent were one-parent female-headed families (and almost 3 percent were one-person male-headed families), and these female-headed families included 17 percent of all children in the Unites States (18 percent in 1978).

The U.S. divorce rate has consistently exceeded that of any other country, doubling between 1965 and 1976 from 2.5 to 5.0 per 1,000 population. It has apparently stabilized at this figure. According to Census Bureau projections, about 38 percent of women now in their late twenties may end their first marriage in divorce. Of the 75 percent who will later remarry, about 44 percent may redivorce. In other words, approximately 40 percent of all current and potential marriages among young women now in their late twenties may eventually end in divorce.[6] Indeed, the number of one-parent, female-headed families has increased at a rate far exceeding that for all other households. Between 1970 and 1977, family households of female householders increased by 37 percent while husband–wife households increased by only 6 percent.[7] Although 48 percent of the wives living with their husbands were in the labor force in March 1977, about 56 percent of the women who headed families were working.

As many as 46 percent of all children born in 1977 are likely to live for a period of at least several months as members of a one-parent family according to an estimate made by Glick and Norton. Although most children under eighteen live with two parents (80 percent in 1976) the proportion living with both of their natural parents who have been married only once has declined substantially to 67 percent in 1976 (and 45 percent of black children of that age).

Clearly, the experience for children growing up in the last quarter of the twentieth century will be very different from that of those who grew up previously. Of the 61 million children under the age of eighteen in 1977, 48 percent had mothers who were either employed or seeking work, and of these 6.4 million were below age six. Seventeen percent of the children in the United States lived with one parent, whereas seven years earlier, in 1970, only 11 percent did.

On the average, black children are more likely than whites to have working mothers (55 vs. 46 percent in 1977). However, there are significant differences by family types. More black children in husband–wife families had mothers in the labor force regardless of the age of the child, while more white children than blacks among those living with their mothers only had a working parent. On the other hand, black children are far more likely than white children to be in a one-parent, female-headed family.

Despite these variations, it seems increasingly likely that the overwhelming majority of children will experience living with a working mother as they grow up, and that close to half will live with their mother *only* at some time as they grow up. For those children who live with their mother alone, the likelihood of having a working mother is, of course, even higher.

Summary

Thus, women are in the labor force and likely to remain there. The overwhelming majority work out of economic necessity. Female heads of families are more likely to work than married women living with their husbands; however, labor force participation rates for married women constitute a truly astonishing development over the last decade. Participation rates for divorced, widowed, and separated persons have stayed relatively constant between 1955 and 1977 for both men and women. Participation rates for unmarried women have increased slightly during that period of time. But for married women the figures are startling. Participation rates rose for wives from 34 percent in 1964 to over 48 percent in 1977; the trend is even more extraordinary for those aged twenty-five to thirty-four, the prime years for childbearing and childrearing. By 1978, half the married women between the ages of twenty-five and thirty-four, living with their husbands, were in the labor market. Indeed, the most significant family and work development in the mid-1970s has been the growing entry into the labor force of married women under the age of thirty-five, living with their husbands, with preschool children in the family. Over half the mothers of school-aged children are in the labor force now. Half the mothers of children aged three to six are working and almost 40 percent of the mothers of children under three.

It is this pattern of women entering the labor force even when they have young children at home—a pattern increasingly common to all advanced industrialized countries—which is creating a social revolution in work and family life in the United States. And it is this phenomenon with all of its implications for daily life, for families, for children, and for society generally, which is the focus of this study.

Wage earning and parenting, carried out as simultaneous roles, will soon characterize most adults, regardless of gender. What will this mean for American families? What will this mean for women who will be the first to have to cope with this major life-style change?

Notes

1. Family support systems are those programs, benefits, measures, or arrangements designed to have—or having—the effect of facilitating, enhancing, helping, or optimizing role enactment of family members and the functioning of the family as a unit.

   Family support systems may be either formal or informal. Formal family support systems are those programs, benefits, and measures explicitly intended to have the effect specified above, while informal family support systems are arrangements such as social networks and personal relationships which have the effect of accomplishing the same goals.

   For other discussions of the significance of family support systems, see Kenneth Keniston, *All Our Children* (New York: Harcourt Brace Jovanovitch, 1977); Urie Bronfenbrenner and Moncrieff Cochran, "The Comparative Ecology of Human Development" (mimeo.); Robert Moroney, *The Family and the State* (New York: Longmans, 1976).

2. Mary Jo Bane's book with its title, *Here to Stay: American Families in the Twentieth Century* (New York: Basic Books, 1976), provides an excellent illustration of this conclusion and the data supporting it.

3. This section draws heavily on data published in *Current Population Reports*; the *Monthly Labor Review*; and the Department of Labor, 1977, Bureau of Labor Statistics, *U.S. Working Women: a Databook.* Specific citations are provided only for particular points.

4. See Ann Foote Cahn, ed., *American Women Workers in a Full Employment Economy* (Washington, D.C.: Government Printing Office, 1977), especially Mary Dublin Keyserling, "Women's Stake in Full Employment"; see also Nancy Barrett, "The Family in Transition" (Washington, D.C.: Urban Institute, 1978), processed; Howard Hayghe, "Working Wives' Contribution to Family Income in 1977," *Monthly Labor Review*, Vol. 102, No. 10 (October 1979).

5. *Current Population Reports*, Series P-60, #114, "Money Income in 1976 of Families and Persons in the United States," July 1978.

6. In addition to the *Current Population Report* reference, *ibid.*, see Paul C. Glick and Arthur J. Norton, "Marrying, Divorcing and Living Together in the U.S. Today," *Population Bulletin* (Washington, D.C.: Population Reference Bureau, Inc.), Vol. 32, No. 5 (October 1977).

7. *Current Population Reports*, Series P-20, #324.

2

Learning About Working Mothers: The Study Process

The Study

THIS STUDY PROVIDES an in-depth look at how a selected group of black and white women in both one-parent, one-earner families and two-parent, two-earner families are experiencing a new and different life-style which is rapidly becoming the modal pattern for all adult women in the United States.

How the study was carried out is the focus of this chapter. What these women are like, what their families are like, including their husbands and children, what kinds of problems they have, and how they manage the complexities of these two demanding worlds of work and family will be discussed in subsequent chapters.

The nature, extent, and implications of role problems for women who are in the labor force and who also have children—and the interrelationship of these problems with community institutions, services, and facilities—is an area of research that has received no attention as yet. Although ultimately large-scale surveys will be essential, what seems needed first is some insight into

17

the kinds of problems that exist as a consequence of the working-mother roles: how women cope in daily living; what their experiences are in using formal or informal family support systems; what the consequences are for children and families of the use or nonuse of different systems. In the long run, both surveys and case studies are needed, but a good starting point is an exploratory hypothesis-generating study. Yet to say "exploratory study" does not specify procedures, instrument development, data collection, and analysis.

The study was predicated on a sample of 200 working mothers with at least one child under compulsory school age. The sample was to be divided equally between two racial groups (black and white), subdivided into each of two contrasting socioeconomic groups (professional/managerial; clerical, service, or other unskilled occupations). The sample was to be representative of the major structural family forms (one-parent, female-headed; two-parent) but weighted more toward the one-parent family than is typical of the society at large. Finally, the women selected were to be in one of the following two contrasting patterns of labor force participation in relation to family roles: (a) continuing to work when first child was born (or after taking a maternity leave of no more than eight months); or (b) entering or reentering the labor force when the youngest child enters school (or a child-care program) or other child-care arrangements are made. In short, this was to be a purposive sample, structured to yield maximum insights but not lending itself to precise quantitative generalizations to any universe of mothers.

For purposes of sample selection, *work* was defined as full-time, paid employment of at least thirty-five hours per week.* Full-time student status and part-time employment with the intention of entering full-time employment was acceptable for participants in the study but limited to only a very small portion of the sample (less than 10 percent).

Continuity of work after childbirth was defined to mean women returning to work at the same job as held prior to child-

---

*The definition of full-time employment used by the Bureau of Labor Statistics.

birth, after a brief hiatus of no more than eight months (two months before childbirth and six months after). This time period was selected because several European countries already have legislation permitting between three and nine months' paid maternity leave. Thus, it seemed a reasonable standard to apply.

Reentry to work was defined somewhat arbitrarily as meaning a hiatus of at least one and one-half years after childbirth, usually involving return to a different job from that held previously.

The final selection of the sample involved some modification of these criteria. Of particular importance, an additional group of women were included: women either just off public assistance or in the transitional stage of working yet still receiving public assistance benefits. In addition, certain *occupational criteria* were selected as relevant for the purposes of the study. A deliberate effort was made to draw upon a variety of occupations and work patterns in order to tap the widest range of needs as well as responses and approaches employed to satisfy these needs. The study deliberately sought out women working different shifts in order to obtain their perspectives. Although women working in their own homes were inlcuded (e.g., family day care mothers, psychotherapists), their participation was restricted. Similarly, teachers and college professors were included as study participants, but also only in limited numbers, since their work schedules are more flexible and offer extensive vacations, thereby attenuating some of the pressures faced by working mothers in other occupations.

More specifically, the sample was divided as seen in Table 2–1.

Approximately two-thirds of the women in the two-parent families were "returning to work" while one-third were in the "continuing work" status. In contrast, among the one-parent families, the overwhelming dominant pattern was one of reentering the work force. The portion of women in one-parent families was particularly high among the lower socio-economic group for two reasons: (1) about half of the women in each subsample are in the "public assistance" group, which by definition means single-par-

TABLE 2-1. Working Mothers Sample

	PROFESSIONAL/ MANAGERIAL OCCUPATIONS N = 97		LOW-SKILLED & SERVICE OCCUPATIONS N = 108		TOTAL N = 205[a]
	Two-parent	One-parent	Two-parent	One-parent[b]	
White	45	7	30	24	106
Black	30	5	38	26	99
Total	75	12	68	50	205

[a]The original plan was to include an additional five women in each sample to offset possible loss between the first and second interviews. Recruitment problems precluded achieving this for the black sample. Similarly, we were unable to obtain precisely the same proportions across racial lines, especially for two-parent families and for "professional" families.

[b]Half the women in this category were recent or current recipients of Public Assistance who were also in the labor force.

ent status;* (2) women's wages, on average, are 59 percent of men's wages; women who head families are likely to have low incomes and these families constitute a very large proportion of the low-income families in the United States.

STUDY SITE

Although several counties in New York, New Jersey, and Connecticut were considered as possible study sites, the final selection was Maplewood County.† Maplewood was chosen because of the wide range of industry in the county, the mix of blue-collar and white-collar female workers, and the interest of community groups in cooperating in the study, Moreover, as a county with a variety of communities within it, ranging from relatively large cities to small suburban towns, Maplewood permits comparisons of need-meeting and problem-solving patterns in areas with both more and less formal resources. As a consequence, a variety of patterns and life-styles could be explored.

*Except for the very small number of two-parent families receiving AFDC-UP, none of whom were included in this study.
†Not the real name of the county.

Finally, the sample was selected through a procedure that holds the place of residence rather than work place constant. This decision was made because primary concern was with utilization patterns of formal and informal resources, not with the characteristics of a particular work place. Moreover, as mentioned above, variety and range of occupation and work place were deliberately sought.

One important reason for selecting Maplewood had to do with the availability of cooperation by both public and private agencies in facilitating identification of a possible study sample. More than 100 such organizations and agencies participated in our recruitment efforts. County agencies, business enterprises, and unions publicized the study and facilitated voluntary participation by individual staff members who met study criteria. Similarly, hospitals, private social service agencies, district school systems, day care programs, women's groups, local colleges, church groups, and so forth were enthusiastic in their support and their cooperation.

STUDY METHOD

This was a panel study in which the women were interviewed intensively on two occasions, about six months apart, for about one and a half to two hours each time. The interviews occurred at a critical point in the adult life cycle, while these women were actually experiencing milestones in relation to their roles. Thus, they were interviewed when returning to work after a brief maternity leave or entering or reentering work after a more extensive child-caring/childrearing leave. The second interview, held six to eight months after the first, was designed to highlight changes and a retrospective review of the experience, as well as to assure the reliability of information provided in the earlier interview.

The research schedule involved completion of the following tasks:

- *Phasing in the Study*, to include: literature and research review; specification of criteria for sample selection; site selection; and selection of cooperating agencies and organizations regarding the sample

- *Instrument Development*, to include: pilot testing of instrument for first interview
- *Field Work*, to include: (1) beginning and completion of first wave of interviews of white sample and preliminary analysis of data; (2) recruitment of black sample and completion of first wave of interviews with this sample; (3) development and testing of instrument for second wave interviews; (4) second wave interviews completed first with white sample and subsequently with black sample; (5) completion of data analysis; (6) report preparation

The study was launched in the beginning of 1976, and field work covered the period between May 1976 through December 1977. Interviewing of the study sample members was carried out by trained interviewers, both full-time study staff and part-time staff. Except for some selected exceptions in the second wave of interviews for purposes of reliability and validity, all interviews of the black sample were carried out by black interviewers. Similarly, the white sample was interviewed by white interviewers. Interviewees were paid $10 per interview, a fee that was fairly standard at the time for interviews of comparable length.

The major difficulty in completing the study within the original time frame projected (two years) had to do with unanticipated problems in recruiting an appropriate study sample. We would have had no difficulty in obtaining our sample quickly if we had been willing to include women who used only formal out-of-home child-care arrangements. Day care and nursery school mothers constituted a large, available pool of interviewees, but we deliberately restricted recruitment of these women in an effort at exploring life-styles and child-care arrangements of women who made alternative, informal arrangements for child care. A second, less important obstacle involved finding one-parent professional families in suburbia. We were told repeatedly that such women were more likely to leave suburbia for central city residences because managing work and family lives for a sole parent is easier in the cities and these women, in contrast to other, less skilled women in similar family circumstances, had adequate incomes to support a comfortable life-style in the city. Finally, our problem in recruiting black participants had to do with the difficulty in finding women who were returning to work. A larger pool of women who were continuing work and not leaving employment following childbirth was more readily available; it took longer to find some women who were returning to work after an extensive period at home.

The instrument used for interviewing these working mothers contains eighty-seven items in eight sections. Three items are for the interviewees' impressions; five are open-ended questions; all others are structured. The major areas covered include the following:

(a) *Family Characteristics*

Race; family type; work status; occupation;* hours of work and length of time to get to job;* income;* marital status; household composition; place and type of residence and reasons for choice; proximity of relatives and frequency of contacts (visits and telephone);* education;* religion;* ethnicity.*

(b) *Work Information*

Reasons for working; attitude toward present job and future employment; job requirements of travel and/or overtime and attitude toward these; use of—or availability of—maternity leaves; attitude toward maternity leave and related benefits; work-related arrangements regarding child care or family emergencies; job history since becoming a mother.

(c) *Child Care*

Age of child/children when mother began/resumed full-time work; child-care arrangements for children under compulsory school age; distance from home of arrangements (when out of home); getting child to care arrangements; reasons for use of present child-care arrangements; satisfaction or dissatisfaction with arrangements; problems in locating satisfactory arrangements; child-care arrangements for school age children; availability of, use of, and attitudes toward after-school programs, school lunch; cost of child-care arrangements; arrangements for care during school vacations; arrangements made in case of emer-

*Asked for both parents, in a two-parent family.

gencies (illness of child or of child-care person, closing of program, etc.); allocation of responsibility for child care within the family; nature of family activities; family/school relationships.

(d) *Household Management*

Types of chores and tasks; allocation of responsibility for household chores and tasks; use of household appliances, convenience foods; responsibility for bill-paying and budgeting; attitudes toward household tasks.

(e) *Recreation/Socialization*

Activities during work week (with and/or without children)—both recreational and educational/vocational; weekend activities, both with and without children; frequency of visits with friends; mother's free time; vacations.

(f) *Obtaining Advice*

Types of problems requiring advice and help; resources used.

(g) *Neighborhood Resources (Formal and Informal)*
Resources other than Child Care

Knowledge about existing resources; use or nonuse of resources and reasons; helpfulness (or nonhelpfullness) of resources; other resources needed; advice to other working mothers; family and community attitudes toward working mothers.

The instrument used for the second wave of interviews also includes a "use of time schedule" for a work day. Each interviewee was asked to fill in a time budget for a twenty-four-hour day (an ordinary work day, excluding the hours on the job) and to provide certain other specified time data. This additional schedule was included as a consequence of findings from the first wave of interviews. A pervasive theme stressed by the women we interviewed had to do with the constant time pressures they experienced—the difficulty in organizing tasks within time constraints and the need constantly to juggle multiple tasks at the same time. We wanted to offer these women an opportunity to provide more detail on this obviously stressful area of a working mother's daily life. Thus, this study has assembled specific information on how these women do spend their time and how they allocate it among tasks and priorities.

In the second wave, only 195 of the original 205 interviews were completed: 103 in the white sample and 92 in the black. Three families in each subsample moved out of the state, and we could not arrange interviews with them. (Two other families who moved were interviewed.) Three other women in the black sample moved from their previous addresses and could not be located; one black woman refused to grant a second interview.

Several changes occurred between the first and second interviews: Three women changed from two-parent to one-parent family status, while one changed from a one-parent to a two-parent family. Two women no longer received any public assistance by the time of the second interview; no others in the sample became recipients. Five women had new babies; ten became pregnant; and one couple had initiated adoption procedures.

The most frequent change, as might be anticipated, was in regard to child-care arrangements. Almost two-thirds of the families changed child-care arrangements during this period. The reasons included: the presence of a new baby and a supplementary care arrangement or a variation of that described earlier; a change in child's age coupled with a new "school" year, leading in several instances to a child's entering a preschool program; a change in season (a second interview during the summer) with different "summer" child-care arrangements; failure of a previous arrangement, either the departure of an in-home child-care person (a domestic servant), or dissatisfaction with a family day care mother, or a change in the plans of the usual child-care person. All such changes as relevant are discussed where the specific material is analyzed.

Working Mothers in Suburbia

Although the women in our study clearly are not a representative sample of working mothers in the United States, or even of working mothers in suburban communities in the United States, we have pointed out that they are not completely atypical. Thus, before proceeding to a more detailed analysis of the kinds of needs and problems these women have and how they manage their daily lives, a brief description of who they are, what they do, how much they earn, and what their families are like may be of interest.

We begin, first, with an overview of Maplewood County. Then we offer a picture of the Maplewood women who constitute our study sample.

MAPLEWOOD COUNTY: AN OVERVIEW[1]

Maplewood is a highly developed suburban county within commuting distance of New York City. The total population of the county is about 880,000, but 70 percent live in the southernmost third of the county, an area which includes several fairly large cities and most of the blacks and Hispanics. About 9.5 percent of the population is black, significantly higher than the national figure for suburban communities generally (6 percent). The largest ethnic minority is Italian, and about one-third of the population is estimated to be of Italian extraction. There is also an Irish population, descended from an earlier immigrant group, as well as a subsantial number of Latin Americans and Greeks among the newer immigrants.

The individual communities range from affluent residential areas populated by professionals and executives to blue-collar working-class communities with extensive light industry, and heavily populated older cities suffering from many of the problems of central cities including the presence of a large poverty population.

The county has about 370,000 jobs. Two-thirds of the labor force work and live in the county. More people commute out to jobs than commute in, but the number of jobs in the county is increasing steadily, as is the size of the labor force. The unemployment rate is about the same as that for the nation as a whole. Similarly, labor force participation rates for women are about the same as for the country as a whole.[2]

There are about 240,000 families in the county and approximately 11 percent are female-headed, significantly less than for the country as a whole. Median household size is 2.9. Median family income for 1976 is close to $20,000, about 20 percent higher than that of the state ($16,105) and 25 percent higher than for the country generally. About 5 percent of the population receive some form of public assistance.

A "Directory of Services for Families" in Maplewood lists 85 agencies as offering individual, family, marriage, vocational, education, recreational, spiritual or crisis counseling and other services. Sixty-five agencies, including a substantial number of the above family-serving agencies, are listed as providing mental health services (out-patient care, day treatment, or partial hospitalization). Nineteen agencies, including some listed in the other categories, provide legal services, and another group of agencies provide service to substance abusers (alcohol, drugs) and their families.

In many ways, the Maplewood Study women are very similar to other women in the same status in any urban or suburban community in the United States. The average size of the household in which they live is three persons. More specifically, with regard to household size:

- 15 percent of the households are one-parent and consist of mother and one child
- 35 percent of the white households are four-person households
- 20 percent of the black households are four-person households
- 10 percent of the white households include five or more persons
- 25 percent of the black households include five or more persons
- 11 percent of the white households and 22 percent of the black households include at least one person outside the immediate family, usually a relative.

Half the families, in both black and white samples, have only one child; about one-third have two children, and the remainder are almost equally divided between three and four children. Only three families in each sample have more than four children.

The age range of the group is also fairly typical of young couples with preschool-age children. Thus, median ages are thirty and thirty-three for the white sample (women and men) and twenty-seven and thirty for the black. Given the fact that twenty-three is the median age nationally for having a first child and thirty for giving birth to a last child, the age of the sample is clearly representative of adults at this stage of the life cycle. These years are peak years for paid employment as well as child-bearing and early child-care responsibilities.

Median length of marriage is six years for the white sample and five for the blacks. It is the first marriage for ninety-eight of the white women and eighty of the blacks. It is the second marriage for five of the white women; three have never been married. For three of the black women, this is a second marriage; sixteen have never been married.

The range of occupations among participants is quite wide. Regardless of race, the professional/managerial subsample includes the following:

- Teacher (primary and secondary school)
- Professor
- Psychologist
- Chemist
- Librarian
- Medical researcher
- Physician (intern, resident, and practicing physician)
- Registered Nurse
- Social worker
- Editor, reporter, writer
- Administrator/executive (government agency, social agency, school, bank, corporation)
- Computer programmer

The clerical, services, and blue-collar subsample include these:

- Licensed practical nurse
- Secretary
- Telephone operator
- Clerk
- Keypunch operator
- Paraprofessional (social worker, teacher, nurse's aide)

- Waitress
- Salesperson
- Factory worker
- Domestic servant
- Family day care mother

Median wages for the white women are $11,400 per annum, and for the blacks, $9,152. The specifics are as follows:

	PROFESSIONAL/ MANAGERIAL		LOW-SKILLED/ SERVICE		One-parent (Public Assistance)	Median
	Two-parent	One-parent	Two-parent	One-parent		
White	$15,000	$14,500	$11,750	$8,320	$7,800	$11,400
Black	12,000	12,000	9,200	8,900	5,400	9,152

As is usual, wage differentials between white and black males are larger than for females. Thus, for the husbands in these families, white males have median earnings of $18,000 per year ($22,500 and $14,300 for each subsample) as against $14,300 ($17,500 and $12,400) for blacks. Family income, although higher than comparable national figures, is not much higher than similar figures for New York State, given the fact that almost all participants in this sample are in the labor force (196 of 205), and most of the families are two-earner families. Thus, median family income for the white sample is $23,200, and for the blacks, $19,500. The range in family income is from $5,300 to $86,300 for the white families and from $6,700 to $60,000 for the blacks. Clearly, two salaries make a difference to family income.[3]

This is a well-educated group, too, something that is increasingly characteristic of younger families in the United States generally. Most of the white women and their husbands are college graduates; most of the blacks had some college.

Finally, for the entire sample regardless of race, the median work week for women is between thirty-five and forty hours per week; the work week for their husbands is forty-one to forty-five hours, with a significant number (25 percent) who define the length of their work week as "varies." About half of these men held two jobs.

We turn now to a detailed picture of how these women manage their lives. We begin, in the next chapter, by exploring how their children are cared for during the day while they work.

Notes

1. The sources for the data on Maplewood County include *The City and County Data Book*, the New York State Department of Labor, the County Planning Department, and the County Department of Social Services.
2. An interesting sidelight is that in 1977, for the first time, the percentage of suburban women nationally in the labor force at 50 percent exceeded the rate for women living in cities, which was 48 percent.
3. Median income in 1975 nationally, for families where the wife was an earner was $17,000, and $19,700 where she worked all year at a full-time job. These figures were higher in 1976–1977 when our study was carried out and are still higher today. See Beverly L. Johnson and Howard Hayghe, "Labor Force Participation of Married Women, March, 1976," *Monthly Labor Review*, Vol. 100, No. 6 (June 1977).

Who's Minding the Children?

3

The Problem

WAGE-EARNING WOMEN who also have children lead complicated and demanding lives. This is something we all understand by now. What is new, for many people, is recognizing that this life-style already characterizes most adult women, and the trend is still growing. For those who are not aware of this development and some of its implications through personal knowledge and observation, the mass media have begun to take account of how American society is changing. Popular magazines and TV shows have begun to dramatize women's lives and problems when faced with the pressures of work and family. A new national magazine, *Working Mothers*, is aimed directly at this group, as distinct from the readers of the more traditional magazines (and even these have changed in content and focus).

Despite many other changes that have occurred, it is generally believed that most working mothers continue to have primary responsibility for their children—and for child care—regardless of whether they are married and living with their husbands or living alone. The extent to which husbands share in housework, household responsibilities, or even child care (when mothers are

31

at home) will be discussed subsequently. The focus of this chapter will be on how women fulfill what has continued to be their major home and family responsibilities even when they work for wages outside the home and even when they work full time. In other words, *how do women cope with child care responsibilities when they are employed full time outside the home?*

In the early 1960s Alva Myrdal and Viola Klein published a revised edition of an earlier work entitled *Women's Two Roles.*[1] Coming at a time when women were beginning to enter the labor force in large numbers, the book found a ready audience. The position taken by the authors in this influential work is one that many have continued to hold even today. Working mothers have two roles, two jobs (only one of which is paid), and although increased sympathy and understanding are forthcoming to women in this position, there is still not much available in the way of real help.

For women with preschool-age children, the situation is particularly difficult. School-age children at least are in school for most of the working day. There are problems, of course, when schools are closed. One-day holidays are bad enough, but some of those are legal holidays at work. On the other hand, the longer winter and spring holidays create special problems for working parents, and the summers represent a potentially even greater strain. There are difficulties, and parents use various solutions, but somehow these seem somewhat more manageable for older children. In contrast, arranging for child care for preschool-age children looms as an insurmountable problem for many women. Subsidized day care centers and nursery schools have limited places and restricted eligibility; private, nonsubsidized programs are often expensive or, at any rate, beyond the means of many individuals. The desire on the part of many parents for a warm, nurturing, and competent woman to care for their child—preferably in the child's own home, and unquestionably for little money—is as forlorn and beyond reality as many other desires. Most warm, nurturing, and competent women are already in the labor force themselves. A few are at home taking care of one or more children of other mothers whose work takes them outside of their homes; but even then the children are not cared for in their own homes.

The U.S. Scene

The problem of child care for preschool children is so complicated in the United States that it is hard even to obtain an accurate picture of how children are cared for during the day when mothers work. Data are not collected systematically and in one place. In general, data series do not recognize the "child-care" functions of preschool and kindergarten. These surveys usually omit educational facilities and report only children in centers and family day care as "cared for" outside the home. The major consumer study of recent years includes casual babysitting and gives it equal weight with extensive regular child-care arrangements.[2] Children up to the age of fourteen are included in most tables, making it impossible to understand how very young children are cared for. Data are not disaggregated for working mothers, clearly an important difference when one assesses types of child care used and amounts of time of such care.[3] Both census and special survey definitions are in transition, however.

The following is the best estimate of current national child-care coverage for children under compulsory school age.[4] The data do suggest a distinctive pattern for children aged three to five. Most organized and formal child care serves this group.[5]

Of the 9.7 million three- to five-year-olds (1976), about half were enrolled in preprimary schools, either nursery school or kindergarten, and another large group (about 11 percent) were already attending first grade. About 1.5 million (15.5 percent) were in centers or family day care and one-third of these already attended some type of school. Adding up the best estimate for an unduplicated count, we get a total of nearly 6.2 million children aged three to five participating in some form of school or out-of-home day care program, or about 64 percent of the age cohort. The overwhelming proportion (59 percent) were in a formal school or center program—largely not all day.

Four million children under the age of three had mothers who worked at some time in 1976, and two-thirds of these women worked full time. The National Infant Day Care Study suggests that 121,500 children under three were in center care. An earlier consumer survey of parents found that 180,000 children of this age were cared for at least thirty hours per week in centers and 364,600 in family day care homes.[6] In addition, 370,000 were cared for in their own homes by a relative other than the child's own parent or by a nonrelative.

The UNCO data suggest that for the under-threes in particular, almost half the children are cared for in their own homes or by relatives, either in the relatives' home or the child's home (55 percent). It seems clear that very few of these children are in group care. The most extensive care, however, what is termed the "long hours" (more than ten hours per week), is clearly day care and preschool and some nonrelative care outside the home (family day care). (See Table A–1, p. 173.)

Maplewood County

Turning now to Maplewood County, what is the child care picture there? There are no good data on where and how preschool children are cared for during the day, when mothers work, in Maplewood County—as there are none for the country as a whole. There are various estimates of children in what is formally called "day care," but these reports ignore the fact that some programs describe themselves as "day care" centers and others call themselves "nursery schools" or child development centers, and all need to be put into the picture.

A recent survey in New York State (whose accuracy cannot be verified) indicates that there are 54 day care centers, 8 prekindergartens, 36 nursery schools, and 252 family day care providers in addition to the public school kindergartens, which offer childcare services and programs for preschool children in this county. The total number of children enrolled in these programs is not clear, however.[7]

An early problem we faced when asking women where their children were during the day while they worked had to do with classifying programs appropriately. After the first few interviews, we realized how important it was to get the exact name of the program, not just the mother's description of it. We found that women use the terms "day care center" and "nursery" or "preschool" (or "school") interchangeably—as do the children who attend, and even some administrators! We were told by several directors that names were a form of "label," and if the label had *cachet*—or, on the contrary, was stigmatized—this would influence the decision to keep or change a program's name.

Indeed, in Europe, the term "day care," in whatever language, is used only to describe the system of child care serving children under three, while "preschool" is used to characterize child-care programs serving children aged three to six. Since these preschool programs operate under the auspices of public education authorities, the label is particularly appropriate. They are expanding rapidly in many countries and serve almost *all* children aged three to six, on a voluntary basis, in several countries (e.g., France, Belgium). Thus, like school, for older children, the preschools have emerged as the primary out-of-home child-care institution. Although this trend is beginning to emerge in the United States too, it is nowhere near as strong in this country, perhaps, in part, because in most of Europe the programs are publicly subsidized while in the United States they are largely private.[8]

The Maplewood women in our study are not a representative sample of working mothers in the United States generally, or even of one state, as we indicated earlier. Nonetheless, details on how they manage this primary responsibility of child care while they are working (and most work full time) offer some interesting insights into both the complexities of their lives and the difficulties inherent in obtaining a clear picture through survey data.

The 205 women in the study have responsibility for 357 children (188 in the white sample and 169 in the black) or 1.7 children per family in each group. Given the fact that these women are still in their prime childbearing years, and several indicated that they expected to have one more child,[9] the likelihood is that over the next few years the average number of children may be close to two per family. But it seems very doubtful that it will be much higher. Of these 357 children, 235 (119 white, 116 black) are of preschool age; 128 (61 white, 67 black) are under three, and the remainder are between three and five.

Assuming that children through the age of ten require some sort of supervision, we explored both the different types of arrangements families make to assure adequate care and supervision while parents are at work, and the extensiveness of use of these programs.

Child-Care "Packaging"

We were struck first simply by the number and diversity of arrangements. Clearly child care, for working parents, means packaging a variety of care modes. The packages often include both in-home and out-of-home care and may even include multiple arrangements, with two types of out-of-home care (group and family day care), as well as two or more arrangements at home, used to care for one child in the course of a week. The amount and extent of parental ingenuity and creativeness are extraordinary, with parents sometimes selecting complicated work schedules in order to provide a significant portion of child care themselves.

Just the logistics of child care for one child, let alone two or more children, often seemed overwhelming, as we heard mother after mother describe multiple and complicated arrangements requiring planning, organization, and reliability. Indeed, one of the most difficult aspects of this approach to child care, as one mother told us, is the "linkage" problem—in other words, getting a child from home to a preschool program, when the program begins after the mother has to leave for her job, or arranging for a child to go from kindergarten to a family day care mother or a relative's home for afternoon care.

The number of child-care arrangements used by families in a typical work week are as follows:

NUMBER OF CARE ARRANGEMENTS	NUMBER OF FAMILIES	CHILDREN UNDER AGE 10	
		No.	*%*
1	76	86	26
2–3	93	148	46
4–6	36	93	28
	205	327	100

The number of care arrangements experienced by each preschool child is as follows:

NUMBER OF CARE ARRANGEMENTS	NUMBER OF CHILDREN	PERCENT OF PRESCHOOL CHILDREN
1[a]	105	45
2	64	27
3–4	66	28
	235	100

[a]Includes seventeen children who are in all-week care or in a special school, or who had nonworking mothers at the time of the interview or were cared for by their mothers at work.

To provide some sense of the extent of this "packaging"—referring to the 327 children under age ten (172 white, 155 black):

- *76 families* (39 white, 37 black) with *86 children* (evenly divided between both groups) use just *one type* of child care.
- *36 families* (21 white, 15 black) with *93 children* (52 white, 43 black) use between *four and six types* of child care.

The remaining 93 families, representing almost half the total sample and 46 percent of the children, use either two or three types of care. Thus, for 129 families (63 percent of the total) involving about three-quarters of the children, child-care arrangements are a package. For these families, child care is a planning, organizing, management, and transportation problem.

What are these child-care packages composed of? What kinds of child care do parents use for their preschool children?

The range or types of care parents use include almost every type that exists in any place in the country. Among these are the types listed below. In addition, four women (two in each group) take their children to work with them; two are family day care mothers themselves; one works in a Head Start program; and another has a special arrangement at work which permits bringing her child with her. In the black sample, one woman has her child in a special school for handicapped youngsters. Two others bring their children to a relative's home for the full work week.

Types of Child-Care Arrangements for Preschool Children

Out-of-Home Care

Group Care:
A.   Publicly subsidized day care centers
B.   Nonsubsidized day care centers
C.   Public-school-based kindergarten
D/E.   Private (mainly not-for-profit) preschools (nursery school, kindergarten)

Individual Care:
F.   In home of a relative
G.   In home of a nonrelative (family day care)

In-Home Care
H.   By father
I.   By other relative
J.   By nonrelative

But "lists" do not quite suggest what all this means in real life.

THE ANDERSON FAMILY: WORKING DIFFERENT SHIFTS

The Andersons are not unique in the pattern they have followed in coping with child care. They work different shifts. Jim

Anderson works a standard 9:00 A.M.–5:00 P.M., Monday-to-Friday work week as a sales manager in a medium-sized corporation. Mary works Saturdays and four nights a week as a telephone operator, a job she told us appeals to many women in her circumstances because it makes it possible for parents to share child care. The Andersons have two children, Jenny, aged one and a half, and Jimmy, Jr., aged four and a half.

On a typical work day for the Andersons, Jim gets up at 6:00 A.M., gets the boys up, washes and dresses the baby while helping Jimmy, if he needs help dressing. He fixes breakfast for the children and himself, cleans up the breakfast dishes, and gets the boys ready to leave. At 8:00 A.M., he takes the children to a neighbor's house, where the four-year-old waits for the school bus to take him to a nearby preschool program. The baby remains with the neighbor. Then Jim leaves for work. By 9:00 A.M., Mary gets back from work, picks up the baby, and returns home. She plays with the baby for a while, makes the beds, straightens up the house, and fixes lunch for herself and Jenny. After lunch, she and the baby nap. Mary usually sleeps in "shifts"; while the baby sleeps and again in the evening after supper. Jimmy comes home from school at 3:30, and the three of them play together for a while. (Sometimes Mary does laundry then.) Then Mary bathes the children and fixes supper for the family. When Jim gets home, they all eat supper together, and then Mary goes to sleep for a while, until it's time for her to get ready for work. Jim takes over the evening routines with the children. Jim has to go out of town on business two days a month. Those nights, his mother stays at the house so they can manage.

This family's child-care package thus includes: father's care and a neighbor's care for the baby; father's care, the neighbor's care and nursery school for the four-year-old—all in addition to what the mother does when she is not at work.

One reason for sending Jimmy to nursery school is that last year, when Jimmy was in a half-day program and stopped napping after lunch, Mary couldn't sleep in the afternoon. She became exhausted and had a bad cough for a while. She then had Jimmy cared for by a neighbor for three hours every afternoon while she napped, but decided it was not a good arrangement for the boy—that he needed more stimulation. Thus, this year they found a good preschool that covers the full school day. She is concerned about next year, when Jimmy enters the public kindergarten, again only a half-day program.

THE JENSEN FAMILY: PAYING FOR HELP

Many people would think the Jensens have an ideal situation; both are physicians, and with their high income they can afford a "sleep-in" who takes care of their six-month-old baby and a three-year-old. But the three-year-old goes to a nursery school in the morning, and the Jensens' schedule is such that they both have to leave for the hospital before it is time for their son to leave for school. The baby is too young to take along regularly, especially if the weather is bad. The Jensens employ another woman just to take their son to and from school, and they have a "back-up" woman if she gets ill.

The child-care package for the infant: one in-home servant; for the three-year-old: nursery school, an in-home servant, and a separate "arrangement" to cover to and from school.

THE REILLY FAMILY: RELATIVES' HELP

The Reillys have a "live-in" child-care person too: Mrs. Reilly's mother. She took full care of the Reilly's two-year-old last year, but this year she has found it a little exhausting, so the Reillys now take Beth to Mrs. Reilly's sister two days a week. Next year they plan to put Beth in a local playschool for the mornings. Mrs. Reilly's sister will pick her up, and her mother will care for her in the afternoons.

The child-care package: in-home care by a relative; out-of-home care by a relative. Next year: add a group "playschool."

JENNIE THOMPSON USES FAMILY DAY CARE—PLUS

Jennie Thompson, who is separated from her husband, works as a secretary in a lawyer's office three days a week. She takes her eighteen-month-old child to a family day care worker—a woman who takes care of three children in her own home. Two other days a week Jennie takes the baby to her aunt's house. Sometimes she has to work on a Saturday; then she gets a teenager to stay with the baby.

The child-care package: a family day care worker, a relative, a teenager.

THE BROWN FAMILY'S COMPLEX PACKAGE

The Browns have two children, a five-year-old in kindergarten and a year-old infant. Both Mr. and Mrs. Brown teach school, and their hours are somewhat easier than those of the working families described above, except that Mr. Brown's school involves a one-hour drive each way, which makes for a long day. Anna Brown takes the five-year-old to a friend's house when she is leaving for work. The friend has a child at the same school and so takes the two together, making it possible for Anna Brown to leave a little earlier and take the baby to a woman who cares for her during the day. The kindergarten is only a half-day, however, so Mrs. Brown has arranged with two different mothers to take her daughter home with them for lunch and part of the afternoon: three times a week with one and two times a week with the other. She picks both children up on her way home from school. In return for this, she takes her friends' children every Saturday for the whole day, giving them lunch and taking them for some special activities or for a day at her house. That day, her husband takes care of the baby.

The child-care package: family day care and father's care for the baby; three nonrelatives (one neighbor; two separate friends); and kindergarten for the five-year-old.

Interestingly enough, the pattern regarding the number of child-care arrangements used for the individual preschool child is similar for both racial groups. More than half the children experience at least two or more types of care while their mothers work, and close to one-fifth are cared for in three or four different ways. Only about 45 percent in each group are in one type of care for the entire time.

Of at least equal importance, the amount of time spent in care does not differ significantly between racial groups. Nor does it vary with the number of care arrangements used. As would seem to be obvious, when women work, young children have to be cared for. When women work full time (and most of these women work between thirty-five and forty hours per week), we would assume that care must be arranged for forty to forty-five hours per week. And indeed, this is what we found.

For the 221 preschool-age children with full-time working mothers or full-time students (excluding those children in all-week care, in special schools, with currently nonworking and nonstudent or part-time working mothers and mothers who take their children to work with them) mean, median, and modal patterns of numbers of hours in care during the week are the same: forty-five hours per week.

More specifically, in the white sample, the 49 children in one type of care only are in care for 43 hours per week; the 39 children in two types of care spend 46 hours in care per week; the 27 children in three or four types of care spend 47 hours per week in care. For the black sample, the 49 children in one type of care spend 45 hours per week in this arrangement; the 41 children in two types of care arrangements spend 46 hours a week in care; but the 23 children in three or four types average only 44 hours. None of these differences are significant. Instead, what is significant is the consistency with which most of these children are in some kind of child care arrangement for about forty-five hours per week, regardless of whether it is one type of care or multiple arrangements.

Conventional descriptions of how children are cared for during the day when mothers work usually seem to imply that many mothers care for their own children or that not much other care is needed. In contrast to such an approach, common sense should remind us that when women work full time, their children must be cared for somehow. Clearly, with very few exceptions, women cannot take care of their own children when they work outside the home, and survey data that report otherwise should be viewed with suspicion. Either the question was asked badly or the interviewer did not understand the response. Asking such questions as, How many hours a week do you work? At what time do you leave home and when do you return? How and where is (are) your child (children) cared for during this time? assures much fuller detail. And it is through the richness of this detail that we began to learn about the problems of child care and the diversity and multiplicity of arrangements, often even within one family for one child.

What Makes a Difference? Race, Family Structure, Class

For both groups, out-of-home care predominates for children in either one or two types of care, while in-home care is the dominant mode for children experiencing three or more types of care. There are differences, however, in the type of out-of-home care favored by each group. Group care is the dominant mode in the *white sample* for families using one arrangement only:

$(N = 49)$

Out-of-Home Care		In-Home Care	
group care	18	parents' care	1
family day care	12	other relative	1
relative care	4	other nonrelative	10

For the comparable group in the *black sample*, the pattern is distinctly different:

$(N = 49)$

Out-of-Home Care		In-Home Care	
group care	12	fathers' care	2
family day care	16	other relative	2
relative care	15	other nonrelative	2

Although family day care and care in the home of a relative are far more prevalent among blacks than whites using multiple forms of care, it is worth noting that regardless of race, the over-whelmingly dominant pattern for both groups, when using mul-tiple arrangements, involves some form of group experience for the child for at least part of the day. Thus, of the sixty-five white and sixty-four black children experiencing multiple care arrange-ments, almost three-quarters (forty-eight white, forty-six black) were in some form of group care for some portion of the day. (See Table A–2, p. 174.)

We turn now to exploring whether or not these patterns vary by family structure or by socioeconomic class.

Here, the most significant finding is that both family struc-ture and social class or occupational status do seem to influence the type of child care used, or at least the dominant mode. Thus, although no significant patterns can be discerned among two-parent families, when we looked for which type of child care pre-dominated, a definite pattern did emerge among one-parent families.

Two-parent families seemed to make equally extensive use of both in-home and out-of-home child care. More important, child-care packages predominate over single modes of care. Of particular interest, some use of group care, either alone or as part of a cluster of arrangements, characterizes two-thirds of the group.

For one-parent families, out-of-home care (group or family care) is overwhelmingly dominant, with 90 percent of the fami-lies using this type of care. Moreover, for two-parent families, group care is used more than any other single form of care, either as the sole form or as part of a package. In analyzing the re-sponses of our one-parent families, three factors emerge as affect-ing their choice of a child-care mode: (1) the lack of money to pay for nonrelative in-home care; (2) the likelihood of having fewer relatives to turn to, to provide such care either in the rela-tive's home or the parent's home; (3) the belief that their children need a supplementary, enriched experience during the day, where they are exposed to more children, different adults, and a more stimulating environment generally. This last factor was mentioned repeatedly in our interviews with these mothers. This belief, coupled with a conviction that only a group center–based program could provide such an experience, resulted in a very high use of such programs by these women. Since family income for many of these women was relatively low, the availability of publicly subsidized child-care programs was enormously important. Indeed some of the greatest concern about restriction in child-care options came from one-parent families where the woman's earnings made her ineligible for subsidized child care, yet not wealthy enough easily to afford market care. For several, choosing such care involved a real financial sacrifice, requiring them to forgo a variety of other necessary expenditures. Yet each who did this felt it a worthwhile sacrifice, to provide the "best care" for her child.

If we differentiate by socioeconomic class or occupational status, the major distinguishing characteristic has to do with more or less use of relative care. Thus, although there is a balanced use of in-home and out-of-home care among the professional/managerial families, nonrelative care predominates overall. In contrast, some form of relative care predominates in families headed by individuals in lower-skill occupations.

More specifically, among the white two-parent professional families, the use of paid domestic help is the dominant child-care mode in one-third of the families and is used as part of a child-care package by about one-half. The pattern is similar, but weaker, among comparable black families, with out-of-home nonrelative care (family day care) playing a significant role.[10]

In contrast, among the working-class families, relative care predominates for both black and white families, whether it be in-home care—often by the child's father—or out-of-home care. Once again, we would hypothesize that the cost or price factor is important in this choice of child care. However, it seems clear that values also play an important role, in the stated preference for having a child cared for by the parents, whenever and wherever possible, or by a close relative. Often, a mother would tell us quite specifically, as Ginna S. did, "I moved here to be near my sister. She said she would be able to take care of Jimmy and he was getting to be too much of a handful for my Mom. Sis takes care of Jimmy (aged two years, ten months) as if he were her own, so I can be relaxed while I'm away at work. No stranger would feel that way about him, no matter what kind of degrees she had. And my husband feels the same way. He said if Edie couldn't take care of Jimmy, I should try to change my hours at the hospital so we could split caring for him between us."

Similarly, Aurelia T., another mother, told us how her mother, Mrs. S., quit her job when Teddy was born, so that Aurelia could keep hers. Mrs. S. felt that taking care of the baby was important; Aurelia's earnings were essential to the family. Mrs. S. had been working part time to supplement a small social security benefit, but both felt better when she stopped work, knowing the baby was in good hands, grandmother's hands.

Thus far, we have addressed the questions of whether race, family structure, or class seem to be significantly linked with any particular patterns of child-care usage. Where this group of working mothers is concerned, *race* by itself seems to make little difference. *Family structure* seems to make some difference, in particular, for one-parent families who appear to use out-of-home care, especially group care, more than any other type of care, proportionately more than it is used by any other group. How much this pattern is the consequence of real preference and how much it results from the fact that these women are likely to be in low-income families, and thus are more likely to be eligible for subsidized group care, is difficult to determine. All we can say is that their stated preference, in addition to actual use, is for group care, for the reasons mentioned earlier.

Class, also, seems to influence child-care modes and the composition of child-care "packages." Here the combination of race and class seems to accentuate the differences. Here too, however, we must raise the question of whether the patterns we discern reflect actual preferences, real even if somewhat limited choice, or only existing availability of resources.

Age Makes a Difference

As we continue to explore the data for further insights into patterns of choice and use in child care, we turn to still a fourth variable: *the age of the child* as it affects or may affect the use of different types of child-care arrangements. Initially, when the study was designed, we were not aware of any particular significance attached to the age of children. All the literature surrounding the day care discussion focused on preschool children from birth to compulsory school entry at age six. Our first awareness that age might make a difference emerged as a major finding of an eight-country cross-national study in which child-care policies and programs comprised one of the six social service fields studied in each country.[11] As we analyzed the individual country reports and prepared our own integrated analysis of the country materials, our most significant finding in the child-care field was that for most of Europe children from age three on were expected to participate in preschool programs, usually free, under public, educational auspices and available on a voluntary basis to all children whose parents wanted them to participate, regardless of whether or not their mothers worked. Indeed, what emerged very clearly is that parents in these countries[12] actively wanted such programs for these children once they reached age three, because they thought them an important supplementary experience for their children.

When the present study was designed, we were not yet aware of the possible significance of age as a determining factor in choice of child-care mode. In any case, this was not the prime focus of the study. However, in analyzing the child-care data and discovering, first, the patterns already identified above, we decided to explore further and test out our hypothesis that age might be a significant indicator of both parental preference and parental choice of child-care mode.

Our analysis suggests that this indeed may be so, although it would require a much more extensive survey to confirm our tentative conclusion. Certainly, any analyses of national use patterns seem to confirm our finding.

Thus, for the 124 children under age three[13] (57 white, 67 black), 55 have in-home care as the dominant form of care, and 27 more are cared for out-of-home, but in the home of a relative. In contrast, of the 107 children aged three to five (62 white, 45 black), 82 are cared for outside of the home in either day care centers, preschool programs, or family day care.

More specifically, 34 attend a day care center; 44 attend a preschool program; and 10 attend a family day care program.[14]

The differentials mentioned earlier hold up in this analysis, too. Thus our white two-parent professional families make extensive use of in-home paid domestic help, and such care is used most for infants and toddlers. Comparable black families use similar in-home help and also family day care, especially. Out-of-home care predominates for the one-parent families, and day care especially for the lower-income families among these, regardless of race. Relative care predominates among two-parent working-class families, regardless of race, for the care of the very young, and continues to be a significant factor in the case of the slightly older child, but only to supplement the more extensive use of group and preschool programs for children of this age. (See Table A–3, p. 177.)

Fathers Help, Too

We described earlier how Jim Anderson shares with his wife the care of their two children. In fact, one of the particularly fascinating findings of the study was the truly astounding amount of child care provided by fathers in the two-parent, two-earner families.

Among the 205 families, 143 (75 white, 68 black) were two-parent families. In 36 percent of these (52) husbands played a significant role in child care, and in 20 percent (28) father's care was the dominant form of care provided. Nineteen families deliberately chose to work different shifts in order to manage most child-care responsibilities by the parents themselves. Often this pattern was selected because close relatives did not live nearby, or the couple wanted to maintain a particularly close and intimate relationship with their child. In six families, the father was unemployed and provided child care for all or a portion of the time while the mother worked. In one family a deliberate decision had been made to reverse traditional roles, at least temporarily, since the wife earned substantially more than her husband had earned when he worked. In another family, the father worked at home and organized his schedule so that he assumed child-care responsibility when the children came home from preschool. In still another family, the father was a full-time student and fitted his parenting tasks into that schedule (or vice versa).

For some fathers, their own schedules made active participation and sharing in child care somewhat easier than for others. Mark S. is a college professor who works at home two days a week. Those days he arranges his work so that he can give eighteen-month-old Jennifer lunch and take care of her during the day. John T. is a full-time college student who works as a bartender Friday and Saturday nights, plus one other night a week. His class schedule lets him take care of his four-year-old son three afternoons a week, picking him up at the preschool program those days, while John's sister takes over on the other two. His wife works from 9:00 A.M. to 5:00 P.M. as a medical researcher.

For other families, the choice of life-style is deliberate and planful. In the Pulaski family and the Scotts', the men are firemen and their wives nurses. Each parent works different shifts, and the men work rotating shifts, too. Each couple also staggers their vacations. In these two families, husbands and wives, with "gap-filling" child care and other help provided by neighbors and relatives, manage to care for two preschoolers while both parents work. One father was present when we interviewed his wife. "There is nothing I can't do for that baby," he said proudly when talking about his nine-month-old son. "After his first three months, when Nan returned to work [after a three-month unpaid maternity leave] he got so used to my feeding him he complained when I left. Now Nan and I split everything: bathing, feeding, changing—it doesn't matter."

In twenty-four families, fathers perform essential child-care
tasks, even though they may not fulfill the primary child-care
role. Among these are the fathers who take children to or from
other child-care facilities or caregivers; fathers who dress and
prepare breakfast for a child when the mother leaves very early
for work; fathers who care for a child evenings when mothers
work late; fathers who care for a child on Saturdays, when
mothers' jobs require Saturday work. In this auxiliary help, in
the primary care fathers share with mothers, which we described
above, and in myriad other ways, fathers are an essential part of
the child-care package used by working parents.

Are Parents Satisfied?

By and large, the overwhelming majority of parents express satisfaction with whatever child-care arrangements they currently
use.[15] Where school-age children are concerned, an extraordinary 90–92 percent of the mothers in white and black families
state that they are completely satisfied with their current arrangements, and indeed only one black mother and one white
mother expressed definite dissatisfaction. Although parents of
school-age children are significantly more satisfied than parents
of preschool children, even among the latter group of parents,
outright dissatisfaction is expressed very infrequently: by three of
the white mothers and six of the black. In contrast, 76 percent of
the whites (78) and 84 percent of the blacks (82) are completely
satisfied with their current arrangements, while 21 percent of the
whites (22) and 10 percent of the blacks (10) have mixed feelings
about the type of care they use.[16]

Most of the complaints as expressed by the mothers interviewed have to do with the high costs of good "child care," especially preschool programs, the strain of coping with complex logistics, or the poor quality of care, usually meaning inadequate
stimulation for the child. Several mothers expressed "mixed feelings" about their current child-care arrangements. Most of these
women mentioned that the child-care costs represented a heavy

financial burden, which for some precluded the use of a group program. Another group of complaints, including some by parents who were bothered about the cost of group programs, had to do with dissatisfaction with family care arrangements, in-home nonrelative care, or even, in two instances, relative care. "My child is bored at her house," one mother said of a family day care arrangement, "but she's reliable and good to him." "There is only one other child in her home," said a mother, "and my boy really needs to play with other children more." On the other hand, another mother said, "The woman who takes care of Linda is just great with kids but she's so good that everyone wants her and she can't say no. She has between fifteen and twenty-four children in her home on any given day and something tells me that's really too many for her to manage alone!" Two women, commenting about their mother and mother-in-law respectively, said, in almost exactly the same words, "Ma is great with the baby but she is just not right for my older boy (one aged three and the other, almost four). She's old-fashioned and doesn't let him do many things and he needs to be more active and to play with other kids." Two parents complained that the public school kindergarten their children attended was excellent but had too short a day, with no lunch. One mother would have preferred a live-in child-care person; one mother objected to the children in her child's day care program; several complained about transportation problems and about the tensions and complicated linkages necessary to keep the whole package working. As one mother said, with great intensity:

"I worry all the time about what I'll do if something goes wrong during the day while I'm at work, or just before I leave in the morning. My neighbor, down the hall, takes the kids with her in the morning when she brings hers to school. The older one [age four] goes to school and the baby [two and a half] is in the same school but just for the morning. I have a very good woman who picks the baby up, takes the baby to her own home and gives her lunch, and later picks up the older one. I pick both children up on my way home from work. My husband works late, so he can't help. If my neighbor is sick—or one of her kids are sick—and I know the night before, I try to find someone else. Otherwise, it means I'll do it myself and be late for work. Thank God I have an understanding boss—and it has only happened once this year. But my fear is that the other woman will have an emergency and may not be able to reach me. She has my neighbor's number for such a problem, and the number of another friend. But neither of those women have cars and the woman's home is two miles away."

Although this woman was expressing her concern about the problems and limitations of the child-care package she had developed, what impressed us most was how frequently this kind of situation was described as typical and how few women complained about it. As we mentioned earlier, by far the overwhelming majority of women interviewed said they were completely satisfied with their current child-care arrangements, even though a large number described situations very similar to the above. As another mother told us, after she completed her description of an unbelievably complicated "typical day," "The most important thing for a working mother with young children is good health and stamina—for her and her children and probably her child-care person."

At a meeting where the results of the study were first reported publicly, we obtained some insight into what may underlie some assertions of satisfaction in the face of what often appeared to be very unsatisfactory—or at least complicated—arrangements. Two young women commented that they were not surprised that most mothers said they were satisfied. "After all," one exclaimed, "the sense of guilt could be overwhelming for some women if they had to acknowledge that their child-care arrangements were not satisfactory—especially if they thought them unsatisfactory for the child!" A second woman, who had been a participant in the study, added a still different perspective: "And if it's unsatisfactory from the mother's point of view, because it's hard on her, that's also difficult to acknowledge. When I was asked that question, I, too, answered that the arrangement was 'satisfactory.' I didn't know it could be any different than it was and I thought I had no alternative, so why complain? In retrospect, that particular 'package' was the worst arrangement I had since the baby was born four years ago—yet I said I was satisfied with it!"

The Cost of Child Care

We turn now to the question of costs. How much do these families pay for child care? Are there significant discernible differences by type of care?

A substantial portion of the total sample (27 percent) pay nothing for the child care they use. Although there is some difference by class (the professional families are more likely to pay; those women moving off public assistance are likely to pay almost nothing), there is very little difference by race and family structure. Thus for thirty families, or 29 percent, of the white sample of full-time working mothers, and twenty-five (26 percent) of the black sample, no cost is involved. About half of these mothers use fully subsidized group care (day care centers, Head Start, prekindergarten or kindergarten in public schools), and the other half use relatives, whom they do not pay, to care for their child, or they use a combination of the two.

A precise analysis of the cost data is difficult and would not appear to lead to any firm conclusion or generalizations, not only because of the size and nature of the total sample but because of the complexity of the issue. For example, although our subsamples distinguish families by race, class, and family structure, we have not controlled for number of children and age of children. Often one such caregiver may be used for two children in the same family at a reduced per-child cost. A number of children aged four and five are in public preschools for a substantial portion of the day at no cost. Our white two-parent professional families have more preschool children than our black families. Those with two or more preschoolers are more likely to use full-time in-home domestic help, which tends to be the most expensive form of child care; however, the cost does cover two children. Mothers found it difficult to allocate the costs of care given

within the home between household chores and child care, or between two or more children who receive care for different periods
of time during the day and week. Some parents also use private
nursery schools for a portion of the day, for one child; this may
be supplemented by in-home care, which is also used for another
child for the full day. In general, families with two or more children pay more for child care than those with only one child, but
not necessarily twice as much.

For those families that pay for their child care, the pattern is
indicated in Table 3–1. Although the numbers are too small to
warrant detailed reporting, we would note in passing that relative care (in own home or in home of relative), government subsidized day care centers, public prekindergarten, kindergarten
and Head Start programs, are the modes most likely to involve no
or very little cost to parents. Nonrelative care in the home or outside the home (family day care) and private nursery schools are
most likely to involve cash payments. Relative care often involves
payments in kind, provision of some kind of services in exchange,
or purchase of food, and so forth.

Paying for Child Care

In exploring the cost of child-care arrangements, we asked also
for the mode of payment (cash, check, or in-kind) and whether
women made use of the existing child-care tax benefit.

Relative care was particularly likely to involve payment in
kind or in some combination of small amounts of cash in addition
to some exchange of services. Almost all of the care arrangements, except the nursery schools and some day care centers
where parents paid monthly or seasonally by check, involved
payment by cash. Much of this, especially when the care was
provided by a nonrelative, operates in a quasi-market economy,
where neither purchaser nor caregiver pays anything in the way
of payroll taxes and the caregiver is unlikely to declare the income.

Despite this, there were a surprisingly large number of wom-
en among those interviewed who were familiar with the child-

T A B L E 3–1. **Total Weekly Median Dollar Costs for Child-Care Arrangements for Preschool-Age Children[a]**
(Only families who incur costs included)[b]
(N = 150)

	PROFESSIONAL FAMILIES				WORKING-CLASS FAMILIES[c]			
	Two-Parent		One-Parent		Two-Parent		One-Parent	
	$	NO.	$	NO.	$	NO.	$	NO.
White	50	(38)	40	(5)	30	(20)	30	(13)
Black	40	(25)	40	(5)	30	(31)	25	(13)
Number of families		(63)		(10)		(51)		(26)

[a]For those families paying for child care. If these costs were presented for the entire sample, including those paying nothing, median costs would be significantly lower, especially for the working-class families.
[b]Fifty-five families pay no money for child-care services.
[c]Public Assistance recipients are not included here. Almost all received fully subsidized child care.

care tax credit[17] and expected to claim the benefit, although our limited discussions did suggest that several women who expressed familiarity with the benefit were less clear about who and what was covered than they had let on.

More specifically, a little over half of both black and white mothers said they knew about the benefit. One-quarter of the whites said they knew nothing about it, and another 25 percent had heard about it but were not sure of its applicability. Over one-third of the blacks were unfamiliar with the benefit, with the remainder among those who were "unsure" about it. Professional families, in both groups, were far more likely to have heard of the benefit and to have explored whether or not they would be eligible. Indeed, once these families are separated out, since the white professional group is larger than the black, there is no difference in the response of the remainder of the women regardless of race. A substantial majority of both black professional women (80 percent) and a clear majority of whites (55 percent) had used or were planning to use the credit, while two-thirds of the blacks and 40 percent of the white working-class families were.[18]

Changes in Child Care over Time

Almost two-thirds of the families in the study experienced some change in child-care arrangements between the first and second interviews. For some women, the presence of a new baby required a different type of care arrangement. A few families moved and changed arrangements as a consequence. For others, the type of arrangement remained the same (family day care or an in-home child care person, for example) but some dissatisfaction—either on the mother's part or on the part of the caregivers—led to a change. Some second interviews took place during the summer months, when special summer programs were used as substitutes for components of the year-round child-care package.

By far the most frequent reason given, however, for a change in child care was the change in a child's age. What this usually meant, for most families, was that a new "school year" had begun and that they had developed a different view of care for their child. Thus, children went from kindergarten to first grade; from prekindergarten or nursery school to kindergarten; from family day care, in-home care, or out-of-home care by a relative to some form of group program. Of particular significance, only one child went from a group program to a nongroup type of care.[19]

More specifically, about half of the forty-five white professional families had made some change in their child-care arrangements by the time of the second interview. In one family, the mother was unemployed by then and was taking care of the child herself. Three families had a new in-home caregiver. Four changed family day care mothers. In a fifth family, the husband, who had cared for the child while he was home and unemployed, returned to work; as a consequence, a family day care arrangement was used. In the remaining seventeen families, the change involved either entry into a group program or movement from one such program to another more suitable to the child's present age.

Among the working-class families, 60 percent changed care arrangements. In this group, too, one mother was now unemployed and caring for the child herself, and one husband returned to work and a family day care mother was used instead. In four more families there was a change in the out-of-home relative providing child care, and in a fifth a new family day care mother was employed. For the remaining twelve families, nine enrolled their children in a "nursery school," one in a day care center, and for the other two families, as well as several of the families with two preschoolers, the change involved "advancing" to kindergarten and/or first grade.

Two-thirds of the black two-parent professional families also changed child care. Two mothers were home on maternity leaves and two others changed their in-home caregiver. Three changed family day care mothers and two changed from family day care to relative care. Ten families changed from one group program to another (day care to kindergarten) or from a nongroup to a group program (family day care to nursery school).

A similar proportion of families changed arrangements among the black working-class families. Twenty-five percent were changes in family day care, while the remainder involved a move to—or a progression to—a group program.

Comparable changes were made in the one-parent families, with one noticeable difference for the group just off public assistance. In several of these families the change involved movement from a day care center to kindergarten or first grade, sometimes with the day care center used to provide supplementary after-school care, and sometimes with family day care used as supplementation.

Summary

Three findings emerge as especially significant from our study of how these working mothers manage child care:

First, when it comes to arranging for the care of their children while they work, these women, regardless of race, class, and family structure, use a varied and diverse group of care modes and, most important, usually develop a child-care package that includes several different types of care. Almost three-quarters of the families studied use two or more types of care, and 28 percent use four to six arrangements. Occasional babysitting for social, recreational, or emergency purposes is not included in this picture, which reflects only the regular "routine" child care used on a weekly basis while the mother works. Although families using multiple arrangements may have two or more children, and the number of arrangements may not be as great for each individual child, the overall picture is still one that requires great management, planning, and coordination skills by the woman and often almost heroic efforts to maintain over a period of time. Furthermore, more than half of the preschool children experience two or more types of care each week, and half of these are exposed to three or four types of care during a routine week.

The dominant form of care may vary depending on family structure or on some combination of race and class; however, out-of-home care of some type is dominant in most of these packages. Group care is used almost exclusively by the single mothers, regardless of race or class. Relative care is an important source of child care in black families generally and in the working-class two-parent families, regardless of race. Fathers play an important role as caregivers, especially in some working-class families, which may deliberately select shift work for one or both parents in order to facilitate sharing child care. Even where fathers are not the primary caregivers, they often provide a significant amount of auxiliary help.

Second, although there are variations in child-care modes among our different types of families, by far the most significant variable influencing the type of child care used is the age of the child. For the three-to-five-year-old children in our study, child care means a preschool program for at least some portion of the day. Three-quarters of the children of this age are attending such programs. Mothers often said that the preferred type of child care when their child was "a little older" would be a "nursery school." Almost all the changes in child-care arrangements for children of this age involved entry into such a program. And finally, although parents with very young children expressed very diverse views regarding preferences for their "under-threes," almost all the parents wanted a preschool program for four-year-olds, and almost as many wished it for three-year-olds. Indeed, a significant number thought their two-and-a-half-year-olds would benefit from such a program.

And *third*, most parents do not make a distinction between day care centers and other types of preschool programs, except perhaps kindergartens based in the public schools. Day care, nursery school, and preschool were terms used interchangeably by parents to describe some sort of a group program. Clearly, what was being stressed by most mothers interviewed was a program that would provide a stimulating and supportive experience for the child—where the child would be well cared for, of course, but where the child also would have an opportunity to develop social and physical as well as cognitive skills. Regardless of the terminology employed, parents want "the best" for their children, and "best," to most parents, means far more than just physical care.

There are other findings, too, which are interesting and warrant further attention, even though they may not be of the same significance as the three mentioned. Of special note is the complexity of assessing what parents pay for child care. For a significant number child care is free, and for another group child-care costs are very low in a monetary sense and may consist of an exchange between relatives or friends. Where there is more than one child, care costs are often viewed as a totality rather than on a per-child basis, and indeed it is frequently difficult to allocate how much goes toward the care of each child.

Finally, we conclude this chapter by noting that the greatest diversity in child care arrangements is in the care used by parents with very young children (under age two or three), but that the greatest number of arrangements per child may be experienced by three-to-five-year-old children who spend a small portion of each day in a part-day preschool program, which then has to be "packaged" with a variety of other arrangements to match the mother's working hours.

Notes

1. Alva Myrdal and Viola Klein, *Women's Two Roles*, 2nd ed. (London: Routledge and Kegan Paul, 1962).

2. UNCO, *National Child Care Consumer Study: 1975* (Washington, D.C.: Department of Health, Education and Welfare, 1976). The most comprehensive supply study is Abt Associates, Inc., *National Day Care Study* (Washington, D.C.: ACYF, DHEW, 1978–79).

3. These data are available but so far have not been analyzed in such a way as to provide answers to the really significant questions.

4. For a more extensive analysis of the important issues in the field of child care in the United States, see Sheila B. Kamerman and Alfred J. Kahn, "Day Care: A Wider View," *The Public Interest* (Winter 1979).

5. Both our estimates and the pattern reported here are supported by a recent article by Mary Jo Bane *et al.* entitled "Child Care Arrangements of Working Parents," *Monthly Labor Review*, Vol. 102, No. 10 (October 1979).

6. UNCO, *op. cit.*

7. New York Minority Task Force on Child Care, *Day Care: How We Care in New York State* (Albany: New York State Senate, Legislative Document No. SO 3216, 1978).

8. For a discussion of child-care programs in these countries, see the chapter on "Child Care," Alfred J. Kahn and Sheila B. Kamerman, *Social Services in International Perspective* (Washington, D.C.: Government Printing Office, 1977).

9. Indeed, six did by the second interview, and ten were pregnant.

10. We would note, in passing, that family day care can be viewed as being closely related to in-home care by a domestic servant; here the child is brought to the child-care person's home, instead of the reverse. Clearly, the cost factor also is important. Whether any other factor accounts for this differential pattern was impossible to discern, from our data.

11. Kahn and Kamerman, *Social Services in International Perspective.*

12. Among the Western countries studied were France, the Federal Republic of Germany, and Israel. Other research in Sweden provided additional data. Subsequently, we reviewed the data for ten other countries in both Western and Eastern Europe.

13. Excluding from this total those categories indicated earlier.

14. There is some overlap here. As discussed earlier, a frequent core package for three-to-five-year-olds may be a part-day preschool program combined with family day care.

15. Such expressions of satisfaction characterize parental responses in other child-care surveys, too. See, for example, Abt, *National Day Care Study*, and UNCO, *National Child Care Consumer Study.*

16. Three white mothers were not included, because one did not respond and two were family day care mothers caring for their own children. One black mother was not included because she was at home on maternity leave, caring for her own infant. This question was asked at the second interview only of those who had changed child-care arrangements.

17. The current child-care tax credit dates from 1975 and was amended slightly in 1978. According to this legislation, child care is a subcategory of "dependent care expenses." The credit is 20 percent of up to $2,000 of care expenses for one dependent and up to $4,000 of expenses for two or more dependents. This gives a maximum annual credit of $400 for one dependent and $800 for two or more. To qualify for the credit (which may be used for either in-home or out-of-home care), the taxpayer must actually incur the care expenses in order to earn income. In the case of a married couple, this requires both spouses to work either at full- or part-time positions, or for one spouse to be employed and the other to be a full-time student or incapacitated. The tax credit base is limited to actual earned income. The 1978 amendment permits the credit to be claimed even if child- care payments are made to a grandparent.

18. In 1977 the credit was claimed for child-care expenses for 4,000,000 children. See Congressional Budget Office, *Child Care and Preschool: Options for Federal Support* (Washington, D.C.: Government Printing Office, September 1978).

19. The same pattern of change as a consequence of children becoming one year older, and more likely to be entering a preschool program, is found in the Abt survey, *National Day Care Study*, as well. Similarly, when parents change child-care modes, the Abt data also suggest that children may be enrolled in a group program as part of the change but almost never transferred from a group program to a nongroup care arrangement.

4

Who Does What at Home: The Changing Roles of Men and Women

THE EXTRAORDINARILY RAPID growth of female labor force participation over the last ten to fifteen years has heralded a major change in American society. Because more women are working, the dominant family form has become the two-earner family. The rise in median family income reflects, in part, the growing contribution made by women to family income. Several studies have reported other significant consequences of this development, as, for example, the fact that almost half of all home buyers in the United States in 1977 were two-earner families.[1] Clearly, although men's earnings continue to be more important in family income generally, women's earnings increasingly make a difference.

We have noted already that although fathers play an important role in providing child care while their wives work, the primary responsibility for selecting and organizing the major part of the child-care package, in addition to "filling in" when emergencies rise, is still the woman's job. Men may participate in deciding how and where a child should be cared for, and they certainly do provide auxiliary help, but the major role is the woman's—indirectly, if not directly.

Now we turn to several other areas of family responsibilities:

- housework and other household tasks, including marketing, cleaning, laundry, cooking, repairs
- child-care tasks and responsibilities when both parents are at home, not at their jobs
- budgeting and paying bills
- decision-making generally, regarding household chores, purchases, recreation

To what extent do traditional sex role definitions continue to determine how these responsibilities are assigned and carried out? To what extent can we begin to see some changes, in particular toward greater equity in the home, as women move increasingly toward greater equity outside the home?[2]

Our data suggest five major conclusions regarding what is happening within the home in relation to household and family tasks and responsibilities. We list and identify them first, before providing details.

First, our data would seem to confirm the decline and almost demise of paid household help to do routine housework.

Second, the traditional division of household tasks along gender lines continues, although significant changes seem to have occurred.

Third, the most significant change revealed in our study is the move from the assignment of exclusive responsibility for tasks to one or another gender, toward increased sharing and role "equity" in the home.

Fourth, we would note that the overall trend and pattern is the same for all two-parent families, regardless of race or class. However, the similarities between whites and blacks are greatest among working class families. Differences, where they exist, seem to indicate that white professional two-parent families may represent a slight variation, not as to the overall pattern but as to the extent to which it is followed.

Fifth, and last, even if nothing else were said about the status of single parenthood, when it comes to household and family responsibilities it is difficult to be a single parent.

Specifics

THE DEMISE OF THE DOMESTIC SERVANT

If anyone still thinks otherwise, our study of suburban families serves as a reminder that the era of paid domestic help is over. Undoubtedly, some domestic servants are still available, and some of our families use such help, but where used (a) domestic servants rarely live in, and (b) they rarely work full time. Where they work full time, they serve a child-care function primarily. Of those families who use such help, most use a once- or twice-weekly "cleaning woman" or a regular "service." Expanded labor force opportunities have provided higher pay, more security, and regular fringe benefits, thus offering many more attractive alternatives to domestic service. Except in the few instances of highly skilled—and paid—cooks or laundresses for affluent families who desire and can afford such help, it is the availability of casual, undisclosed cash income that seems to make domestic work still acceptable to many of the women. And they are clearly a rapidly declining group.

None of our one-parent families and none of the two-parent working-class families, regardless of race, use any paid help for any part of household work. Very little such help is used by the black two-parent professional families. Only among the white two-parent professional families does the use of paid domestic help to do housework assume any significant role, and even among these families almost all such domestic servants provide child care too, often being viewed primarily as child-care givers, and only secondarily as doing housework. To be more specific:

- 75 percent of the white families and 90 percent of the black families use no paid help for household chores.
- 17 percent of the white families and 4 percent of the blacks

use some paid household help, but the help provides a combination of child care and housework services.

- 8 percent of the whites and 6 percent of the blacks employ someone just to do housework.

WOMEN'S WORK, MEN'S WORK, OR SHARED WORK?

Gender continues to play a significant role in the assignment of household tasks and responsibilities in two-parent families. Women are still largely responsible for what has to be done inside the home, and men for the outside work. Despite this, according to what the women we interviewed say, some change does seem to be occurring. Many woman told us specifically that their own households were different from their parental homes and, frequently, different from their own "before the baby was born" or "before I went back to work." Where there is change occurring, however, it does not seem to involve a matter of role reversal but rather a movement toward an increase in joint role fulfillment and shared roles.

We asked a series of questions with regard to such standard, routine household tasks as:

- marketing
- light cleaning
- making beds
- heavy cleaning
- laundry
- cooking meals
- washing dishes (or cleaning up after meals)
- household repairs

For each task, we asked, "Who does this, *most of the time* (husband, wife, either/both, someone else, usually_____)?" Our responses indicated that for all except "household repairs," women continue to carry major responsibility for completion of these chores. With few exceptions, in between 50 and 75 percent of all the families, these tasks are viewed as the women's responsibility. No more than a maximum of 15 percent of husbands accept sole responsibility for any of these tasks, and a substantial number of men never—or hardly ever—help at all. However, of particular importance is that for at least 10 percent of the families and, in several instances, for as many as one-third of the families, many of these are viewed as shared responsibilities.

The details follow below:

MARKETING

Half the women in both black and white families state that they have primary responsibility for marketing.

One-third say that the responsibility is joint.

In between *10 and 15 percent* of the families, it is the husband who takes primary responsibility for marketing.

LIGHT CLEANING

In *half* the families, it is the women who do the daily cleaning.

In *none* of the families do husbands have primary responsibility for this work.

In *one-third* or more of all families except the white professional families, routine housecleaning is a shared responsibility. Among these white families, 25 percent use paid household help for this task, while it is shared work for 20 percent.

MAKING BEDS

Here the consensus is overwhelming, although the pattern is similar to the above.

In *two-thirds* of all families, making beds is the woman's job. Women have this responsibility in only half the white professional families.

In almost *none* of the families do husbands assume primary responsibility for this task.

In *10 percent* of the white and *15 percent* of the black families, it is a shared task. Paid household help in 25 percent of the white professional families do the work that wives do in the other families.

HEAVY HOUSEWORK

Here, for the first time, we see a significant increase in husband's participation. How much reflects traditional gender views of masculine physical strength and feminine fragility is difficult to know. Regardless, for:

- 25 percent of the white professional families
- 50 percent of the white working-class families
- 45 percent of the black professional families
- 35 percent of the black working-class families

heavy cleaning is the wife's job.

For 10 percent of the white families and 15 percent of the blacks, heavy cleaning is the husband's job.

For 25 percent of the white families and 35 percent of the black families, it is a shared job. In almost 40 percent of the white professional families paid help is responsible for heavy cleaning. Other relatives help out in several black working-class families.

LAUNDRY

This, too, is viewed primarily as a women's job. For almost

- 50 percent of the white professional families
- 67 percent of the white working-class families
- 50 percent of the black professional families
- over 75 percent of the black working-class families

laundry is a woman's work.

Despite this, 10 percent of the husbands in both black and white professional families do most of the laundry, most of the time. In 15 percent of the white professional families, over 25 percent of white working-class and black professional families, and 10 percent of black working-class families, doing the laundry is a shared task. Paid help is important here, too, for 25 percent of the white professional families.

COOKING

This is largely the woman's job, although it is a shared task in a significant number of families. For

- 75 percent of the white professional families
- 50 percent of the white working-class families

- 50 percent of the black professional families
- 67 percent of the black working-class families

women do most of the cooking, most of the time. Only among the white professional families do as many as 10 percent of the husbands cook almost all meals.

In 10 percent of the white professional families and about one-third of all other families, cooking is shared between husbands and wives.

WASHING DISHES AND CLEANING UP AFTER MEALS

This is largely a woman's job, although husbands help out more with this chore than with many others.

In both black and white families, 50 percent of the women say that "doing the dishes" is the woman's job in their families.

In the white professional families, 20 percent of the husbands, and in all other families 10–15 percent, assume primary responsibility for this task in their families.

In over 33 percent of all families except the white professional families (and in 15 percent of them), it is a shared task.

HOUSEHOLD REPAIRS

Here traditional gender roles appear once more, with two-thirds of the men assuming full responsibility for all household repairs—the traditional "man's job" in the house. Furthermore, this proportion is consistent for both black and white families regardless of occupational status. Only between 10 and 20 percent of the women say they are largely responsible for this task, with about 15 percent indicating that it depends on the nature of the repairs. For them, this is a shared task, with husbands doing some repairs and wives doing others. An interesting sidelight on the "sexist" assignment of the task here is that in our one-parent families, 75 percent of the women said they did all such tasks, with only the remainder indicating that for this household work they got help.

When it comes to the broad range of *child care responsibilities* within the home, when both parents are home and not at work, a strong pattern of sharing emerges regardless of race. In only a small minority of these families are these responsibilities primarily the woman's. Bedtime is a shared task, alternated between parents depending on time, preference, and so forth, in almost two-thirds of the professional families and half of the working-class families. Playtime with children is shared in 75 percent of the professional families and two-thirds of the working-class families. Either helping a school-age child with homework is shared (with each parent helping some of the time), or father is mainly responsible in 75 percent of all families. Clearly, in a wide range of miscellaneous child-related tasks fathers are active participants, and according to many of their wives, much more so than their own fathers were.

Although mothers come to the fore again when it comes to *caring for an ill child*, in over one-third of the families husbands and wives share equally at such times, while in half the families it's primarily mother's job to take care of a sick child.

It is worth noting here that when it comes to losing work time to care for an ill child at home, about two-thirds of all the women in our study, regardless of race, family structure, or class, did not miss a day in the previous three months of work; 15 percent lost one day and 10 percent two days.

Perhaps the most conclusive finding of all, regardless of specifics, stems from the response we got when we asked our interviewees, "Overall, who do you think is *really* responsible for the children on a day-to-day basis? Who is responsible in the event of a crisis?" Once again, the response was uniform, across race, family structure and class; half the women said they were, primarily, and half said both their husbands and they. For these women and for half the families in our study, childrearing, at least, is a joint responsibility.

Moreover, many of the women we interviewed told us explicitly that as a consequence of their returning to work their husbands became much more involved with the children and much more helpful, generally, at home. Others indicated that since they both had worked all their married lives, the decision to have a child and the anticipatory planning before childbirth was largely a joint effort. Although only some felt their husbands were as fully active and supportive as they had hoped, most viewed their relationship as different from earlier historical patterns of marriage. As one woman who worked as a waitress put it: "There's no getting around it. Bringing money into the family makes a difference. Pete treats me differently now. And he treats the baby differently. Somehow we're much more like partners now." The findings of our study suggest that indeed there may be a real change occurring in two-earner families today and a growing trend toward intra-family equity in adult roles, and toward norms of parenting rather than of just mothering and fathering.

THE DiCARLOS: A TRADITIONAL FAMILY

The DiCarlos seem much like families of an earlier generation, except for the fact that there are two wage-earners in the family, whereas in earlier years there would have been one wage-earner and one at-home housewife.

Teresa, Mrs. DiCarlo, works as a legal secretary. She returned to work six months ago after more than seven years at home when her younger daughter, Tonia, aged four and a half, entered kindergarten. Teresa gets up at 6:00 A.M., showers, dresses, and goes downstairs to prepare breakfast for her husband and two daughters: orange juice, toast, eggs, fresh coffee. At 7:00 she awakens the girls and the seven-year-old helps the four-year-old get dressed. Teresa responds to any of several crises and sometimes reminds the girls they musn't dawdle. At 7:30 the girls come down for breakfast, and Joe, her husband, follows a few minutes later. By 8:00 Joe, a salesman, leaves for work, and at 8:15 the bus stops for the children. After the children leave, Teresa puts the breakfast dishes in the dishwasher, cleans up the kitchen, makes the beds, and straightens up the house. She drives to her job and begins work at 9:30.

Tonia, the four-year-old, is picked up at noon by Teresa's sister, who has a younger child at home, too. Tonia stays at her aunt's for the afternoon; she has lunch there, rests, and plays outside. Her mother picks her up at 5:45 P.M.

Maria, the seven-year-old, goes to a friend's house after school. The friend's mother keeps an eye on both girls while they do homework and play, until Teresa picks Maria up on her way from work, before stopping for Tonia.

By 6:00 P.M. Teresa has collected the two girls and reached home. The girls are sent upstairs to bathe and get into pajamas, while Teresa gets dinner ready. Joe arrives home at 6:30. He usually spends about fifteen minutes with the girls before dinner is on the table. Dinner is finished by 7:30 or 7:45. Sometimes Joe helps Teresa clean up after dinner, and sometimes he plays with the girls and puts them to bed. Teresa says this is the only real change since she returned to work. Before then, Joe would watch TV after dinner and Teresa would finish in the kitchen and then put the girls to bed. She says Joe has really tried to "help," and his offer to help with the dishes or put the girls to bed is a very big change for him.

Teresa usually does laundry two times a week in the evenings, after dinner. While the machine is going, she prepares Maria's lunchbox for the next day. Often, even after she has finished the chores, the girls are still up and want attention. She may read to them briefly or sit and talk.

The house rarely quiets down before 10:00. The DiCarlos go to bed right after the 11:00 news on TV.

On Saturdays Teresa does the weekly marketing, and the girls accompany her. Her husband, who handles all the bill-paying for the family, gives her household money for this and for other personal expenses. She, in turn, gives him her whole paycheck. Teresa usually cleans the house more thoroughly on Saturdays, too. Sundays, the whole family goes to church in the morning and to visit relatives in the afternoon.

Teresa seems quite content with her household arrangements. She likes her job and says that returning to work will make it possible for them to buy a house of their own in a couple of years. (White, working class.)

THE PHILLIPS FAMILY: TOWARD EQUITY IN THE FAMILY

The Phillipses are both social workers. Ron is assistant director of a local "Y," and Cleo is on the social service staff of a large hospital. Cleo received a graduate degree in social work (M.S.W.) two years before she met Ron two and a half years before they were married. She has worked steadily since then, taking off only three months following the birth of each of their two children, aged eighteen months and three and a half years.

The Phillipses manage by a complicated amalgam of sharing tasks, obtaining help from relatives and neighbors, and being well organized and very flexible. Cleo works late at least one night a week, and Ron has meetings to attend two or three evenings a week, but they have managed to arrange their schedule so that one of them is always home in the evening. Cleo is home, also, one morning a week. That is her time to clean the house and do laundry. Ron takes the three-year-old to nursery school in the mornings and frequently picks him up at 3:00 P.M., when school ends, and takes him to a neighbor's house. On the days he can't be there, he calls another neighbor, who picks the boy up instead. Cleo drops the baby off at her sister-in-law's, on her way to work. On the nights Ron is working late she may pick up the three-year-old and they all may have supper at her sister-in-law's. Some nights, if Ron has a meeting, he will come home first and take Cleo and the kids out to MacDonalds for supper. Other nights, whoever gets home first will start supper and the other, later, will get the children ready for bed. Ron works at least one day each weekend. The other day they do different kinds of things, always including the children.

The Phillipses are quite casual and relaxed about who does what. Somehow, Cleo says, the important things all get done. (Black, professional.)

THE FERRISES: COPING BY BUYING HELP

According to Jean Ferris, Sarah Brown is the cornerstone of the Ferris household. Jean and her husband are both lawyers. They have one son, Mathew, aged two. Sarah Brown came to work for the Ferrises when Mathew was three months old, after his special baby nurse had left. Sarah Brown lives with the Ferrises from Sunday night to Friday night; she leaves when

Mathew goes to sleep Friday evening and returns late Sunday evening, having spent the weekend with her daughter and her family.

Mrs. Brown takes complete care of Mathew during the week. She does light cleaning in the house (makes beds, dusts, and so forth) and gives Mathew his meals. Some evenings she even prepares dinner for the Ferrises; however, they tend to eat out frequently during the week and work late several nights each week. Once a month a man comes to the house to do the heavy cleaning. Mrs. Brown also does the marketing.

On the weekends, the Ferrises take care of Mathew, although sometimes they use a babysitter, especially if something special is happening on a Saturday night. Sometimes on the weekend, they entertain friends at home. Jim Ferris is even more likely to cook on those occasions than Jean. The Ferrises try not to work on the weekends, but if either has to the agreement is that the other takes care of Mathew.

Next year, when Mathew is three, he will go to nursery school in the mornings, because the Ferrises feel he needs to be with other children more. But even then they plan on keeping Mrs. Brown with them. She is reliable and good with Mathew, and he loves her. Besides, they are thinking about having a second child. (White, professional.)

WHAT ARE THE CRITERIA FOR DECIDING WHO DOES WHAT AND WHY?

Having described a pattern of household roles and responsibilities in which traditional sex roles are still maintained but gender equity plays an increasingly important role, we turn now to *how women view their intrafamily decision rules*. What are the guidelines by which decisions are made regarding who does what at home? Who decides what the family or family members should do, or buy, and what is the basis for giving priority to one spouse or another, or to a balance between them?

GENDER IS NOT THE BASIS

Fewer than half the women in our study think that these decisions in their families are made on the basis of gender. As one woman lawyer said, "Traditional sex-role divisions would be absurd when I earn as much as my husband does. Our reasons might not seem rational to an outsider, but they have nothing to do with maleness and femaleness." She is among the 75 percent of the black and white professional families who say sex is not a significant factor in decision making in their families.

From a totally different perspective, we quote a nurse married to a policeman, both of whom work different shifts in order to share almost all needed child care between them. "I don't understand this women's lib thing, and neither does my husband. Sure there are differences between men and women. But that has nothing to do with what we do. We want a house of our own and we can't get one unless I'm working. We want the best kind of care for our son and we think we can do a better job between us than anyone else." And then Mrs. A. described one of several different "typical" or "normal days"—since they vary depending on her shift and her husband's shift, both of which change over time. She gets up at 5:30 A.M., bathes, dresses, changes the baby, and feeds him. Before she leaves at 7:15, she wakes her husband up. This week her shift is 8:00 A.M. to 4:00 P.M.; her husband's is 4:00 P.M. to midnight. He takes care of the baby during the day, feeding and changing him as necessary, playing with him and talking to him. Before he leaves at 3:00 P.M. he brings the baby to a neighbor who keeps him for about two hours until Mrs. A. has returned from work. Depending on which shift each has, her husband is as likely to cook, clean, do laundry, and change and bathe the baby as she is. It never occurs to them to decide who does what because one chore is "a woman's job" and another, a man's. They are adults; they have aspirations for a particular life-style, and a fairly modest one at that. They wanted a family—one child now and another in three or four years. They are trying to be good parents and considerate spouses, and how else can you do this except by sharing responsibilities and alternating who does what, depending on who is there, who has time, who can manage. The important thing is the baby and themselves, and they are very clear about who and what they are and how to get where they want to be. They are among the two-thirds of our working-class families, both black and white, who say sex doesn't matter when deciding who does what.

WHO HAS TIME AND WHO IS AVAILABLE

Underscoring the implicit position taken above, only one-third of the women interviewed said that special "skills" or competences influence role and task assignments in their families, while only one-quarter or less think that "interest" or "liking" a particular task should be the deciding factor.

Our study sample seemed to be composed of a highly pragmatic group of women. Between two-thirds and three-quarters of all the women interviewed, regardless of race or class, said that the deciding factor in assigning household responsibilities was who had time and who was available. Implicit in this balanced, common sense approach to household and family tasks is the concept of equity, mentioned earlier. Indeed, for between half and two-thirds of our white and black samples, an equitable division of responsibilities is the overriding principle of role division. In some families this led to more traditional role assignments for some tasks but more flexible views and more nontraditional assumptions about others. It all depended on how individuals and couples felt.

The women who were satisfied with the arrangements in their families were those who felt the division was equitable, regardless of the specifics of who did what, when. The women who were dissatisfied, unhappy, frustrated, and feeling overburdened were not necessarily those who actually *did* any more than other women. Nor were they necessarily those whose husbands did less than other men. But they were, in all likelihood, women who felt that they were overburdened *in relation* to their husbands, that their husbands were not pulling their weight, were not sharing in what they viewed as a joint experience. The repeated plaintive cry heard again and again from both black and white women regardless of class was "It's just not fair," or "It doesn't seem fair," or "Do you think he's being fair?" To say that life is not fair is no answer. Everyone knows that the world isn't fair, but an implicit criterion for a satisfactory work, family, and intrafamily life seemed to be, according to many of the women we interviewed, some sense of fairness between husband and wife—equity in the family.

WHO BUYS WHAT AND WHY

The decision rules regarding financial expenditures involve: expertise, preference, the size of the expenditure, and the extent of direct impact.

Thus, food purchases are usually made by the women, because they are assumed to have some expertise (especially since they do most of the cooking). Preferences for different types of food can be taken account of easily, and an error on one marketing trip can be corrected on the next. Yet, regardless of its being viewed by one-half to two-thirds of the women as their responsibility, in 10 percent of the families husbands do all the food shopping and in about one-third it is a shared (or alternated) responsibility.

Buying clothes is another task that devolves mainly on women. Not only do the overwhelming majority of women (90 percent) buy their own clothes, usually by themselves, but about 75 percent buy their children's clothes, and a significant number (15–20 percent) buy their husband's clothes for him; about one-third shop with their husbands for his clothes, while only half the men shop strictly for themselves, when it comes to clothing.

The pattern changes sharply when we move to more expensive purchases, or expenditures and decisions that focus more broadly on the family unit as a totality rather than individual family members.

More than three-quarters of both black and white professional families decide jointly on purchases of household appliances or a car. In contrast, women play a more significant role in working-class families when it comes time to decide on purchase of a major household appliance, while males in these families play a more active role in deciding on the purchase of a new car.

Finally, when the time comes to consider purchasing a new home, the decision to do so, as well as the ultimate choice, is a joint decision in between 80 and 95 percent of our families.

Similarly, where family recreation and vacations are concerned, decision making is shared equally by husbands and wives. Whether it is a weekend activity or a special "once only" trip planned three years ahead for that year's annual vacation, decisions are shared and plans made jointly, according to most of the women whom we have interviewed.

If decision making in these families reflects an increasing pattern of sharing and jointness, patterns of bill paying seem to reflect both equity and diversity. That is, except for some slight differences, the prevailing pattern with regard to which spouse has major responsibility for paying bills is as follows:[3]

Each pays his or her own personal bills (e.g., clothing, gasoline, repairs on the car, depending on who uses the car most, or for families with two cars, each pays for his/her own), and pays for those bills related to his/her area of primary responsibility (e.g., women pay food and child-care bills; men pay household repair bills).

Where major expenditures are concerned (rent, mortgage, vacation, new car, refrigerator) in about one-third of the families, the women pay all the bills. In another third of the families, the men pay all the bills, and in another third of the families all bills are paid jointly.

Unfortunately, when we explore this pattern, all is not quite as it seems. That is, ideally, we would think this the ultimate in equity—or individual preferences. The reality is that the patterns may not reflect individual preferences, in particular in those families where either women or men are dominant in their roles. Some women told us in rather stereotyped fashion, "My husband says I have no head for figures. My husband pays all the bills." In several families, even though they worked full time and made a significant contribution to family income, the women did not even have personal checking accounts. They handed their paychecks, uncashed, over to their husbands, who in turn doled out "small sums" for household and personal expenditures. One woman said that each morning, before she left for work, her husband gave her money for lunch that day! If she wanted to go out with some co-workers after work, she had to ask for additional money in advance and be prepared to explain why it was a "worthwhile" expenditure. The reverse pattern characterized some other families, with the man handing his checks over to his wife. Some women accepted the pattern, whatever it was, and others resented it. Neither race or class, nor for that matter education, seemed to correlate in this sample with any particular patterns of budgeting and financial management. All we can say with certainty is that an equal proportion of families follow each pattern; most find it acceptable; the others are no more sure how to obtain greater equity here than they are in the arena of family decision making and family responsibilities generally.

SINGLE PARENTHOOD: UNCONFLICTED DECISION MAKING, BUT THE COSTS OUTWEIGH THE BENEFITS

Single parents are spared the conflicts regarding "who does what?" and "what should we buy?" Single parenthood may be never having to explain "why" to a spouse (although there may be twice as many "whys" to respond to from a child). But here for the first time one gets a sense of some of the constraints on the single parent and some of the special problems.

Several of the wives in our two-parent families felt overburdened, overextended, and inequitably treated. But if we look at the total sample of two-parent families, it seems clear that a significant percentage of these women have husbands who share in at least some of the tasks and responsibilities of child care, child-rearing, and household chores. In contrast, one-parent families almost by definition are highly unlikely to have anyone with whom to share any part of their responsibilities. Occasionally, a single parent might have a regular or sometime-cohabitant friend who may be helpful—or a relative, friend, or older child who can help with the baby. But most have no one whom they can depend on regularly, or whom they can turn to even in a crisis. Certainly it's true in many families that if the wife doesn't market there's no food in the house; if the wife doesn't cook, there's no dinner on the table; if the wife doesn't do the laundry there are no clean clothes; and, most serious of all, if the wife is late picking the child up at nursery school she is greeted by a hysterical child and an angry teacher. Furthermore, she may have to deal with a critical husband as well as a critical boss.

However, from what we have learned from our sample, most two-parent two-earner families no longer operate in such an extreme mode. Some families do, but in a growing number intrafamily roles are changing, moving toward equity, out of necessity. Even traditional, authoritarian men are realists; they may not relinquish their absolute power easily, but they relinquish some power when they recognize they have no alternative. In most families in which the woman's earnings are essential for the family's economic survival the men understand the need to share, and indeed often want to. In short, in these families, intrafamily roles are changing and becoming more balanced, more interchangeable, and more equitable.

For the one-parent family, this change is irrelevant unless the family status shifts to two-parenthood, because the single parent has no alternative role.

When Sandy, one of our white single mothers, talked to us about what it was like coping with an active two-year-old as a single parent, it sounded overwhelming. With long blond hair pulled back in a pony tail, wearing blue jeans and a heavy sweatshirt, she looked more like sixteen than twenty-six. Her husband left her a year ago, and she has received no support from him except for twenty dollars at Christmas. Her mother, who lives two blocks away, has tried to help her, but since her own husband became ill she has little time or energy for help, let alone money. Sandy works as the office manager in a law office and makes a good salary, but it's still only one salary and it barely covers necessities. She lives in a one-bedroom apartment, selected because she can walk to work and shopping. She has no car. Her two-year-old, Caroline, is in a day care center, and the fee is partially subsidized. Because the day care center is not within walking distance, and Sandy has no car, she has arranged with another mother who lives not too far away to pick up her child and bring her home at the end of the day. Sandy gets up at 6:00 A.M. five days a week, in order to get the baby and herself ready by 8:15, when the child is picked up and Sandy leaves for work. If she's going to work late and therefore going to be late getting home, she phones the woman during the day and asks her to bring Caroline to her home, waiting for a call from Sandy to tell when she has arrived. Sandy pays for this "extra" child care by the hour, in addition to paying for gasoline for the car, for the transportation to and from the center.

Most evenings, when Sandy comes home she bathes the baby first, gets her in pajamas, and then they play for a while. Then Sandy fixes supper and reads to her daughter. Housework and laundry are done occasionally in the evening, but usually Sandy says she's too exhausted to do much. The only real cleaning is once a week on the weekend. She hates the look of "sloppiness" but says it's hard to manage even straightening up during the week. Marketing is a Saturday task for which she takes the baby with her. If the weather is bad or the baby has a cold, it is a problem. Another problem is that the director of the day care center thinks parents should be "participants" and visit the center for parent meetings several times a year, but this requires a sitter to stay with the baby, and that's not part of Sandy's budget. Sometimes her mother sits. The health clinic has Saturday hours, which has made bringing the baby for a checkup possible, but there are always other problems around schedules. It's hard to arrange for repairs if something like the washing machine breaks. Last week the baby was sick and Sandy couldn't get out even to market. She's just asked a friend to sit for a couple of hours, in return for her doing it with the friend's baby, another time.

It is in this arena of tasks, chores, and responsibilities that we first begin to identify the extra burden of this type of family structure. For these families, extra-family supports become particularly important, be they informal, natural support systems or formal supports. We turn now to exploring how all the women cope with their jobs and the work place, before assessing the support systems they use.

Notes

1. United States League of Savings Associations, "Homeownership: Affording the Single Family Home" (Washington, D.C., 1977). For further discussion of the implication of the growth in two-earner families for home ownership, see Bernard J. Frieden, "The New Housing Cost Problem," *The Public Interest*, No. 49 (Fall 1977), and William Alonso, "Metropolis Without Growth," *The Public Interest*, No. 53 (Fall 1978).
2. For the concept of "equity" as applied to the intrafamily roles of men and women, see Rhona Rapoport and Robert Rapoport, *Dual Career Families Re-examined* (New York: Harper and Row, 1977), pp. 362–364, and "Men, Women and Equity," *The Family Coordinator*, Vol. 24, No. 4 (1975).
3. There are many patterns of separate or joint checking accounts. Here the focus is on control and/or handling of the families' expenditures and financial obligations.

Managing Work

5

EVEN WITH THE accelerated growth in female labor force participation over the last twenty years, the traditional "in and out"
pattern for working women remained fairly constant until very
recently. That is, young women worked until they were married,
or perhaps even when they were married, until they had a child.
Then they withdrew from the labor force for some years while
their children were young, only to return to work once their children were in school. As we mentioned at the beginning of this
report, this pattern began to change in the 1970s. The first important development was the increase in the labor force participation rate of young married women with preschool-age children; increasingly, even those with children under age three. A
second important development, emerging only in the mid-1970s,
seems to be a change in the pattern of labor force attachment for
women in their prime childbearing and early childrearing years.
When we review labor force participation rates of women by
year of birth and age, following cohorts born between 1931 and
1950, this trend emerges quite clearly.[1] Thus, the older cohorts
all stopped working in their mid-twenties; labor force participation rates then declined and only returned to the rate of the earlier period about ten years later. For the cohort born between
1931 and 1935, it was not until 1970, when these women were

between thirty-five and thirty-nine, that their labor force participation rate equaled their rate of work in their early twenties. For those women born between 1936 and 1945, it took until they were between thirty and thirty-four to reach their earlier labor force participation rate. But for the cohort born between 1946 and 1950 we see a significant change: an almost flat line during their twenties, with no decline in labor force participation rates for women between the ages of twenty-five and twenty-nine, the prime years of childbearing for women in the United States. If this pattern continues for subsequent cohorts it would herald a major change in labor market behavior for women and a major change in work-family life-styles. In essence, such a development would mean that women are leaving the labor force for only very brief periods of time—for childbearing but not for child care and childrearing.

Our study suggests this new pattern characterizes our sample. Moreover, study findings suggest some issues, problems, and implications resulting from this development.

Labor Force Attachment

Our initial criteria for selection in the study sample included one variable having to do with whether the women were continuing work, with a very brief hiatus after giving birth to a child, or whether they were entering or reentering the labor force after several years at home devoted to child care and childrearing while their child or children were very young. We had hoped to select a group of women representing a fairly equitable balance between these two different life-style patterns. We had some slight difficulty when we recruited our white sample but ended up with a reasonable balance. When we began recruiting our black sample, however, we found that most of the black professional women we encountered had worked throughout their adult lives and had not withdrawn for childrearing at all. Thus, it was particularly difficult to recruit such women who were entering or reentering the work force. This was not a problem in recruiting black working-class women. In general, if we had limited our sample to women who were continuing work after childbirth, we would have found it easier to recruit the entire sample quickly, rather than trying to include women who had stopped working for two or more years and were now returning.

Our most significant finding regarding how working mothers manage employment and the work world is that clearly these women are committed to the labor force. They need the money; they like being part of the work force; and there are jobs available. However, unlike what we saw emerging within the household and inside the family, we see little evidence of change in the work world, as these women experience it, that would indicate greater responsiveness to child and family demands. When men work and women are at home, family and children's needs are taken care of by the at-home spouse. When women work as the sole parent, or when both parents of a two-parent family are in the labor force, there is no one at home to take care of these needs. Some needs can be responded to outside of work, and, as we have seen, husbands are increasingly sharing responsibility for tasks that used to be viewed as the woman's job before she too entered the work world. But other needs cannot. As men and women increasingly combine parenting and wage-earning roles, it would seem that some adaptation would have to be made both by adults in their parenting and family roles and employers at the work place. Thus far what we have seen in the way of adaptation and adjustment seems to indicate that families are adjusting parenting to the world of work, rather than the labor market's and industry's responding to the parenting and family needs of their employees.

We begin now with some specifics.

The overwhelming majority of the women we interviewed (80 percent or higher), regardless of race, class, or family structure, stated that they expect to be in the labor force indefinitely. "For the foreseeable future," "For the rest of my life," "Until I drop," "Until retirement," "As long as possible," were the phrases used most frequently by women responding to our question: How long do you expect to work? When do you think you will stop working?

Among those women who did not expect to continue working throughout their adult lives the most frequent responses were: "Until I have another child," "Until I return to school," or, for two single parents, "Until I remarry."

When we asked women whether they would work if it were not financially necessary, 60 percent of the professional women, regardless of race or family structure, said they would. Seventy percent of the working-class single parents said they would. Several stressed the importance of work for them as an essential social institution. As one woman put it, "Work is the only place I get a chance to talk to another adult. It's what keeps me sane." Even among those who did not answer in the affirmative, almost all responded by saying, "If I didn't need the money so badly I'd work part-time." Having a little more time at home, for a single mother, would make an enormous difference to several women. Perhaps of particular interest is that 75 percent of the black public assistance recipients and two-thirds of the whites in similar status stated that they too would work, even if it were not essential for financial reasons.

A somewhat different picture emerges, however, when we look at our two-parent working-class families. Only one-third of the white women and a little more than 40 percent of the blacks said they would work if they didn't need the money. Some said under those circumstances they would prefer part-time work, but a significant number, representing the same proportions as said they would work regardless, stated quite positively that if money were not needed they would *not* work.

When it comes to job satisfaction, somewhat surprisingly the professionals seemed to be less satisfied with their jobs than the other women. One possible reason may be that women whose primary reason for working is the need for money may expect less gratification from work, even though work may still be an important and satisfying part of their daily lives. The professional women were clearly career-oriented and many expressed drive and ambitions regarding career advancement. Their frustrations seemed to reflect the comments of the majority who described their attitudes toward their jobs as "mixed." The reasons were very similar regardless of whether they were black or white and often were expressed in very similar terms.

"Too little money for what I do" was a frequent complaint as was, "There's no real challenge to the job. It's just a job and the pay is okay, but it offers no excitement." Another frequently repeated comment was: "There's no real chance for advancement. It's close to home and it's convenient, but I'll have to look for something else soon, because I can't go any place in the company from this job." Other complaints ranged from one woman's frustration with coping with a large bureaucracy to another woman's resentment at the four-hour daily commutation to an excellent job, which she loved, but which was now beginning to seem not worth the strain of the commute. Many of the women in the study said that they accepted less satisfying jobs in order to be near home or to obtain some flexibility in hours.

When asked why they worked, the overwhelming response by 75 percent of the women was, "for the money." This response was even more positive for black women and for working-class women regardless of race. Thus, although 60 percent of the white married professional women said they worked primarily for money, two-thirds of the black professionals said they did so. Almost 90 percent of both black and white working-class women gave the same response. Many women indicated that personal fulfillment and socialization were important reasons for working also, but the real stress and priority, as indicated, was first and foremost on working as a financial necessity, because their families needed the income.

As part of our further exploration of why these women worked and what role their earnings played in the family economy, we asked, subsequently, what use was made of their earnings. Were their earnings earmarked for certain special budget items? Were they part of overall family expenditures? Did they segregate their earnings for personal use? (See Table A–4, p. 181.)

For twenty-four families (twelve white, twelve black) the woman's wages were the sole source of family income. This number does not include those women who were receiving public assistance, because these women described their earnings rather as "major source of family income," with public assistance (and child support in a few cases) as supplementary income. It does, however, include six two-parent families in which the husbands were unemployed.

Women's wages represented the major source of family income, equal to more than half total family income, for eighty-one families, or 40 percent of the sample, including the single women receiving supplementary income from public assistance. In seventeen of the black two-parent families and twenty-one of the white families, the women earned more than their husbands. In eleven additional black families and six white families, the women's wages represented an equal contribution to family income. Thus for 60 percent of our sample (122 families) the women's earnings were essential to the economic wellbeing of the family; the women were responsible for half or more of family income. In sixty-four other families wives' earnings are used to pay the rent, the mortgage, food, medical bills, and other essentials. In only nineteen of the families, 9 percent of the entire sample, are the women's earnings used solely for personal expenditures, for such "luxuries" as the family vacation, or for "special" occasions.

Parenting, for most of these women, did not create a significant obstacle in fulfilling routine work responsibilities. In contrast to the conventional wisdom regarding high absenteeism among working mothers, 67 percent of the white mothers and 60 percent of the black women did not lose a single day of work during the three months prior to being interviewed. In general, most women in two-parent families missed less time than sole parents: 75 percent of the professional wives and 68 percent of the working-class wives lost no time at all, while this was true of only half the white single parents regardless of occupation. The reverse occurred among the black women: Only half the wives, regardless of occupation, lost no time at work, while among the single parents 80 percent missed no days. Including those who missed only one day of work would characterize 75 percent of the sample. Clearly, these women are not casual about their work responsibilities.

Jobs and the Work Place: No Adaptation to Parenting

Although mothers are increasingly in the labor force, and fathers have been so always, the conventional view has been that work and family are separate domains—or, if not, that it is reasonable to expect that work may influence family life but not the reverse. Clearly, this is how the women in our study view the work–family relationship. Managing work means managing job demands and responsibilities despite the extensive demands of home and family. "Not only do bosses not want to hear about problems at home," one mother said angrily, "but women with children continue to be at a disadvantage when looking for jobs, because the assumption is that child-care responsibilities will interfere with work."

HOW MOTHERS VIEW THE DEMANDS OF THE WORK PLACE

Jennie L. is a registered nurse who works on the obstetrical and gynecological floor of a large hospital. She has a nine-month-old daughter who is cared for part of the time by her husband; since she works a late shift she is able to manage child care herself for another part of the time. When her hours overlap with those of her husband, his sister takes care of the baby. Jennie complained to us about the fact that the hospital provided no paid maternity leaves, although it was considered "progressive" and a very good place for women because it does give a three-month unpaid leave with full job protection, seniority, and fringe benefit coverage. "I would have taken off more time if I could have. Six months is what I wanted, but they would only give me three and I need the job. We need the money and basically it's a good place to work. But it's a funny thing working here on this floor. The staff and the attendants all talk about the importance of the early years, especially the baby's first year.

They tell their patients that all the time. Yet the administration acts as if we nurses didn't exist or didn't matter. According to them we should be grateful they let us take any time off! The fact that we get no pay for that time and that it's a hardship for many is denied and certainly the fact that some of us would like to take a little more time off is not even considered."

"Nobody cared and nobody noticed. They asked nothing. I called in sick when my pains began. Then I went to the hospital and had my baby. I was home in four days and one week later back at my job. My Ma is taking care of the baby for me now, when I'm at work." This was the matter-of-fact statement by a single parent, describing how much—or how little—time she had taken off when her baby was born.

"I don't like the job much. It's dull and doesn't pay too well. But the boss is very decent," said another single parent who works as a wrapper in a large store. "He let me use my sick leave and vacations so I could take six weeks off when the baby was born. And he never asks any questions if I call in sick, even though he knows I'm as healthy as a horse, but the baby has had a lot of colds this winter and if he's very sick I can't take him over to the woman who takes care of him."

"I'm fed up with the personal questions, the sneers, the sarcasm, the contempt," said an elegantly dressed young bank vice president. "By the time I was interviewed for this job I just said I had no children and didn't intend to have any. Although I got a raised eyebrow, that was it. It's a lie of course. We have two children, but I got disgusted with being asked questions such as, What does my husband do? Why am I working if he's a lawyer? How do I plan to arrange child care? Don't I feel guilty about working when the children are young? No man gets asked those questions even if he's a single parent! And you're caught between a rock and a hard place. If you get angry that's a mark against you, and if you don't respond you're viewed as inadequate any-way. When I was interviewed for this job I knew I wanted it and I was perfect for it. I decided my personal life was my own and therefore from the bank's point of view I have none. There is something wrong though with having to do this."

"The best part of this job [teaching] is that I have off the same holidays as both children. I could take off a year [with no pay] each time I gave birth. I have compromised on what I thought I would be doing now, but I'm glad I had this kind of a job. Not every woman is in this position."

MATERNITY LEAVES

Almost 60 percent of our sample (119 women) continued work after the birth of their youngest child, in contrast to the remaining group (86 women) who either entered the labor force—or more usually reentered the labor force—after a hiatus of two or more years following childbirth. For those defined as "continuing work," this meant that no more than eight months elapsed between childbirth and the return to work, even though the return was not necessarily to the same job.

Only sixteen women (13 percent of the 119 eligible women in our study) received any paid maternity leave. Their leaves ranged from two weeks to six months, with six weeks both the modal and median amount of time taken. Payment ranged from half to full wage replacement. Another 15 percent (eighteen women) were able to use a combination of personal sick leave and vacation benefits to cover one to six months' paid leave following childbirth. Among those who had the longest leaves were teachers who managed to schedule childbirth so that they could use their summer vacations along with accrued sick leave as a paid maternity leave. Six other women had unpaid maternity leaves but were entitled to full job protection and fringe benefit coverage for a fixed period of time ranging from six weeks to three months. In short, only about one-third of those women em-

ployed at the time of childbirth had any kind of protection related to a maternity leave.

It is worth noting that all except one of the women with some
form of maternity leave benefit returned to the same job at the
end of the leave. On the other hand, more than one-quarter of
the remaining women returned to new jobs, either because taking the leave was grounds for dismissal or, more frequently, because they felt no obligation to return to an employer who had
given them no assurance regarding their job.

Although we cannot draw any firm conclusions from the experiences of these women, certain aspects of their behavior in relation to maternity may be of interest.

First, among all our family "types" those women, both white
and black, who had been public assistance recipients were the
group least likely to have been in the labor force before childbirth
or to have continued work after childbirth. One question that
could be addressed is to what extent does AFDC function as a
kind of child-care allowance for low-income single mothers or as
an extended paid maternity leave for these mothers, and what
are the implications of this?

Mary L., a black single mother and AFDC recipient whom
we interviewed one month after she began working, responded
to the question of why she worked by laughingly saying, "Which
of your reasons means 'not for money'? I guess you could say
I work for 'fulfillment,' because it's sure not for money. I got
almost as much from welfare when I stayed home and did
nothing."

Reinforcing this, from a different perspective, is Linda F., a
white single working-class mother who had become a public assistance recipient between the first and second interviews. "I
couldn't take the hassle anymore. The work was hard, the pay
lousy and I couldn't seem to get a steady child-care arrangement.
First I had one neighbor care for the baby for part of the day and
my mother for the rest of the time. Then my mother got sick and
my neighbor moved. I found another woman in the building, but
I discovered she had eight or ten kids in a small apartment. The
kids never were outside and the baby—who's just a doll—just
didn't seem to look right. I stopped that arrangement fast, but I

had to take three days off from work until I found someone else.
This woman was great, and I was so relieved for three months,
but then she told me she had decided to take a regular job and
wouldn't be caring for kids at home anymore. The baby [now
seven months old] has been moved to five different people since
he was born, and now I had to find a new sitter. I woke up one
morning and thought the hell with it. I'll go on welfare. It's a
crummy way to live, but if after a while they can get the baby in
a decent day care center I'll be back to work. It's not that I can't
get a job. I can. But what I saw happening to the kid was killing
me, and I couldn't figure a way out, and what difference does it
make? Certainly not in the way of money."*

Second, the prevailing pattern for a post-childbirth leave was
six weeks; the expressed preference was for six months. Three-
quarters of the women continuing work after childbirth took off
between one and six months, with the remainder scattered between one week and nine months. When asked, most women responded that a six-month paid leave would be ideal, with some
suggesting that it would be good to have the option of taking a
longer period, if they wished, even if it were without pay. The
single working-class women took the shortest leaves of the whole
group, because, as several said, they could not manage without
their salary. Thus, three of these women were among those five
who took less than one month off.

Five women managed more easily than they might have because their husbands used their own vacation time to help out.

Several women said they wished it had been possible to go
back to work first on a part-time basis, gradually returning to
full-time work.

"You just don't know how much of an adjustment is needed
when there's a baby in your life for the first time. And on top of
that you never seem to get enough sleep. I was tired all the time,
and waitressing is hard work physically. I expected to stay home
for six months or so, but my husband lost his job and we just
couldn't manage without my bringing home a paycheck. With
his unemployment check, I think I might have tried part time at

*Three months later, with her baby placed in a good day care center,
Linda returned to work.

least for the first month but they wouldn't have me unless I worked full time." This was from a young woman who went back to full-time waiting on tables in a luncheonette near her home, three weeks after her baby was born.

CARING FOR A SICK CHILD AT HOME AND OTHER CHILD-CARE EMERGENCIES

One pervasive concern for the women we interviewed was how to manage when a child-care emergency arose. Two women had long lists of "crisis helpers" in case a child became ill—or the caregiver became ill. Either of these constitutes a real emergency, and none of our samples have a benefit that entitles them to paid leave for such a purpose.

"I guess we're lucky. My mother lives nearby and will help out in a crisis. If she can't make it, Jim's sister usually can. Since the baby was born, one or the other has always been available."

"Last year was a nightmare! Jimmy, my older son [then aged three and a half] began nursery school for the first time and caught everything that was going around. There's no way we can keep the kids apart; they share the same room. So just as Jimmy was getting better, the little one [aged two] would come down with it. The whole winter was one long mess of sore throats, ear infections, and at the end—mumps! Bob's mother came to stay for a while, but then she had to go home. I took off some sick days and Bob did too. It was hell!"

"I was going to put my boy [aged two] in a day care center, but they only take kids if they're well. My friend said even with a running nose they make the mothers take them home. Last year he had a lot of colds, but my neighbor took care of him anyway. She's working now at a regular job, and I thought I'd use a day care center, but I can't afford to take time off every time he has a cold, so I guess I'll look for another woman to take care of him until he grows out of getting sick so much."

The routine response when we asked how women managed child-care crises was: "I take a sick day," or "Either my husband or I take a sick day." Several women worked where there was entitlement to a few personal days during the year; they could use these for crises. Although many of the women said it was openly known and accepted at work for women to use personal sick leave benefits to cover child-care crises, especially child-care illnesses, several said it was actively frowned upon at their work place, and they were forced to lie about it. One young woman who worked as a secretary to a woman professor at a university said, "My boss is a bitch, but I need the job. She knows all the girls here use their own sick leave if their kids are home sick. But she told me she'd report me if I did that. So of course I lie. I have a friend call in with some sob story about my having a twenty-four-hour bug or something. The only time I'll have trouble is if I really get good and sick and run over the sick leave I have."

The astonishing thing, of course, as we mentioned earlier, is how, despite their very real problems and fears, the majority of the women interviewed had lost no time in the previous three months because of family emergencies.

VACATIONS

Ten percent of our total sample and 15 percent of the husbands had no paid vacation benefit. The percentage was the same for black and white women but higher for the white than for black men, apparently because several of the white males were self-employed professionals who felt that they could not take time off. Although the amount of vacation benefit varied for the women in our sample from one week to the two summer months and school vacations (for the teachers), most women (75 percent) received two, three, or four weeks. Whereas by far most women said they would vacation at the same time as their husbands if they could, in most families husband's and wife's vacation benefits were sufficiently different so that total vacation time did not coincide. In some families vacation times were arranged by the employer and, as a consequence, were completely different for husbands and wives.

The most frequent variation was that spouses had different length entitlements to vacation time. Teachers, of course, have a full summer vacation lasting two months; college professors have three months; and both have various additional school holidays off. If only one spouse is a teacher, obviously his/her vacation will be much longer than the other's. However, this is true also for a whole series of jobs where vacations range from two weeks to six weeks.

About two-thirds of the women in our sample had a different length vacation from their husbands'. Some had more time, some less, but as a result one spouse always spends a portion of his/her vacation alone. If the spouse with a longer vacation is the woman, that additional time tends to be devoted to children, home, and family. The same is true for some men, although a significant percentage are described as using that extra time strictly for their own personal interests. Regardless, for these families, the overlapping time tends to be viewed as a family vacation, whether the whole family goes to visit grandparents or other relatives, take a trip, or just stay home and relax (and save money).

In about 10 percent of the families, parental vacations from work are at different times, although the women said they would prefer them to be the same. In four families no choice was possible: The man was required to work during the summer; the woman was required to take her vacation in the summer. In some families the husband had no choice and the wife said she often adapted to her husband's schedule, as long as there was some overlap with a school-age child's vacation from school.

Several women said they and their husbands used some vacation days during the year to take time off from work if a child (or a caregiver) were ill.

The issue of coinciding vacation benefits is less important for the parents of very young children than it is for the parents of preschool or school-age children. For many very young children, the care arrangement used during the year was also available during the summer. In contrast the school-age child needs a different arrangement for the summer months, and this did present problems for many families. "No one seems to understand that if you're a working mother the job doesn't stop for July and August, or between Christmas and New Year's. My husband and I each try to get a couple of days around the children's Christmas vacation, because with three children aged three, six, and nine, when school is closed someone has to be available to care for the kids. Most sitters don't want to work over Christmas, or they charge extra, so usually my husband and I divide up the time and each of us takes off a couple of days. When the summer comes we have three weeks off. We manage with the kids because they spend two weeks with my parents, two weeks with his, and then we usually hire one or two teenagers to sit or take the kids to the community pool. If it weren't for the grandparents, I don't know how we'd manage." Indeed, for several of the women, especially the single parents of preschool and school-age children, family was an important component in summer child care. For those who had no available relatives, the summer could present a problem, although there was little consensus as to the nature of the problem, or for which children. Some women complained that there were inadequate activities and facilities for the school-aged, while others thought plenty existed for the slightly older children but provision was inadequate for the younger ones.

In any event, as women become attached to full-time, all-year employment, the length of the vacation benefit as well as its scheduling will become increasingly important.

Summary

As more and more married women with young children enter the labor force, the tension between work life and family life increases and becomes more visible. Women are increasingly behaving like primary rather than secondary wage-earners. They are not withdrawing from the labor force during their childbearing and childrearing years, except very briefly at the time of childbirth. Although internal family roles seem to be becoming more flexible and to be adapting to changing family life-styles, which now include work and parenting for both adults, the same has yet to occur in the work place. Industry has made little if any adaptations to (a) the influx of married women with children into employment or (b) the pressures on male employees as their wives demand that they too share in family responsibilities which impinge on work (or vice versa). No statutory provision in the way of paid maternity leaves exists in the United States. Fringe benefit coverage is sparse and uneven in coverage and entitlement, and little attention has been paid to this issue by organized labor. Far fewer of the study sample had benefit entitlements than is supposed to be the national picture. Moreover, entitlements to paid leave to care for an ill child are practically nonexistent in this country, as in our sample; at best parents use, as these mothers told us, their own sick leave and vacation benefits. Finally, the problem of child care, even for school-age children, remains an issue when school vacations and work vacations do not coincide. This issue is exacerbated further when parents cannot manage their vacations to cover children's vacations, let alone for the whole family to manage at least a reasonable amount of that vacation together.

Note

1. U.S. Department of Labor, Bureau of Labor Statistics, *U.S. Working Women: A Databook* (Washington, D.C., 1977).

6

Family Support Systems:
Natural Helping Networks
and Community Resources

The Problems of Working Mothers

WE ASKED THE same questions in a variety of ways: What is the most important problem for working mothers? What do you worry about most? What advice would you give a fellow employee who is pregnant and says she expects to continue working after her baby is born? What advice would you give a friend who has a young child and says she's thinking of returning to work? What is the most needed resource in your community? What have you found to be the most useful service in your community?

Regardless of which way the questions were posed, and regardless of the race or occupations of the women responding, the basic answer was always the same: *Child care is the central problem and concern of working mothers*. When child-care arrange-

99

ments are truly satisfactory, a large burden is removed from these women's daily lives. Otherwise, it is a constant source of tension.

In addition to child care, the most important problems in daily living have to do with (a) the shortage of time in which to get a variety of family and home-related chores completed; (b) the lack of help at home in fulfilling these tasks; and (c) the pressures of an unyielding work environment in the face of all their child and family responsibilities. These four often unresolved problems lead to a situation of constant stress, for working mothers, with little expectation of relief until children are older and better able to take care of themselves, as well as to participate in other home and family responsibilities.

Yet, despite what appears to be a situation of great strain and stress, these women all seem to accept the situation almost as if it were inevitable, as if nothing can be done about it except to live through it. Remarkably few women complained to us. Those who did complain tended to focus on specifics:

"You'd think the baby was just mine and not my husband's too. He never helps even though he knows I work the same hours he does." (Black, two-parent, professional.)

"There are day care centers for low-income families and nursery schools for the rich but there's nothing for working-class families like us. We wanted Scott to go to a day care center or a nursery school where he could play with other kids. But our income is too high for one and we can't afford the other. Neither of us are really happy about the sitter we use. She takes good care of Scott and I don't mean to criticize her—but he's obviously bored and he says so. We do all kinds of things with him on the weekends, but it's not enough. But it's the best we can do for now until he's old enough next year for the public school pre-K program." (Black, two-parent, working-class.)

"I used up all my sick leave this year when Jennifer had tonsilitis. Last week I went to work even though I had a terrible sore throat and a fever. I just couldn't afford to lose any pay. My supervisor didn't say anything, but I knew she understood. She sent me home in the middle of the day after I had been marked in." (White, one-parent, public assistance.)

When we asked women about personal or family problems—what kinds of problems they had, where they went if they needed help, whom they talked to about their problems—most of the women focused on very concrete problems, if they mentioned any at all.

Several women stated that they had no problems. "And even if I had problems," one white teacher said, "I believe in solving one's own problems." For some women, even acknowledging any difficulty in what looked to an outsider like a tension-ridden situation seemed to imply some personal inadequacy which they were not prepared to reveal. These women believed they had to manage regardless of the situation, because this was "the female burden."

Some, with much more insight, took a very different perspective.

Jane, a speech therapist working at a nearby school, commented thoughtfully, "Only women who have tried to cope with both roles—mother and working woman—can understand the constant sense of tension and fragmentation, the overwhelming complexity of living in constant uncertainty. And the sense of responsibility is enormous. I know how I feel. I'm like the ballast in a ship—what keeps the family on an even keel and what keeps it going. Most women end up doing both jobs all by themselves, even if they are married, because too much effort is needed to initiate a more equitable division. As much as I love my husband, my child, and my job—this is an enormously demanding way to live and often ungratifying because there is little recognition or appreciation from anyone—even from a husband like mine who's really a very good husband!" (White, two-parent.)

Or the forthright response by Celia, a medical technician whose husband was unemployed and clearly depressed at the time of our first interview, "Sure there are problems. But it's not the same when you are working. There isn't time to sit around and think about your problems all the time, or how terrible things are. Work gives you a chance to get away for a while, into a different routine. You come home and maybe things look a little different or you see them more clearly. Will has always worked. He'll have a job again. In the meanwhile, we'll manage.

We always have and it's even easier now with my bringing in regular money." (Black, two-parent.)

And then there were women like twenty-nine-year-old Jeanne, the superwoman who held a high-level position in an advertising company and managed a household that included her husband and two children, a house that always looked spotless, and a role as hostess and wife to a successful young attorney. And with all this, she never seemed harassed. "I may have problems at work, but not at home. Who has time for problems?" she asked laughingly—and only a little flippantly. "It's all a matter of being organized—within an inch of my life." (White, two-parent.)

Although, obviously, not every problem was listed by each of our interviewees, the basic list, for those acknowledging the existence of problems, included all or some of the following:

- Money
- Childrearing and child development (for young children)
- Child learning (for the school-age child)
- Marital relations
- Family (parents, siblings)

Although not viewed exactly as a "problem," when asked whether there were any times of the day or week that were especially difficult, women talked especially about the problems of the interface of work and home. The most frequently mentioned "hard times" were: leaving home to go to work, coming in the door after work, handling an emergency in the middle of the day or just before leaving in the morning.

THE PROBLEMS OF DAILY LIVING: HOW MARRIED
WOMEN COPE

Pat S., the Patient Care Coordinator at a local hospital, described a typical working day in winter. She wakes up when her alarm clock rings at 6:00 A.M., leaves for work at 9:00, and begins work at 9:30. Her work day ends at 5:30 P.M., and, since she usually works a little later, she normally isn't home until 6:30. Bedtime is 12:30 A.M. Her husband has to go out of town frequently for his work and is usually away three or four nights a month. When he's home, he helps get the children ready in the morning, but this was one of the days he was away. Pat has two children, a girl aged two and a half and a boy aged five.

"Out of bed at 6:00 A.M. with a start. No heat. Shivering, I looked at the thermometer—52 degrees. I called for furnace repair, dressed as warmly as possible, and went to the baby just as she woke up, bundled her like a stuffed animal, saw that Bobby was still sleeping, and went downstairs to make tea and hot chocolate. Gave Susie breakfast and made lunch for Bobby. Put Susie in Bobby's room while he got dressed and I went out to shovel snow and start car. Went back inside, helped Bobby finish dress and made beds. The repairman arrived and fixed furnace. Kids played in my bedroom while I took a quick shower, redressed and got them ready to go. Called work to say I'd be a half hour late. I walked Bobby to where the school bus stops. He goes to kindergarten. Then I walked to my mother-in-law's, to leave the baby there. Then on to work, only fifteen minutes late. Called the sitter who picks Bobby up after school. Asked her to check home first and make sure it was warm enough, otherwise to go to my mother-in-law's with Bobby and call me." (White, two-parent.)

Theresa S. is one of the women who shares child care with her husband. She works at night as a telephone operator, so that she can spend most of the day caring for the children herself. They have one twenty-month-old at home and a seven-year-old who attends the local elementary school. Theresa is also trying to complete her B.A., on a part-time basis, so she can qualify for a better daytime job once the youngest is in school. She has completed about half the credits she needs. Her usual day involves getting up at 6:00 A.M., school from 8:00 to 9:30, leaving for work at 7:30 P.M., returning at 2:00 A.M., and in bed by 2:30. She also works one day on the weekend. A typical weekday goes something like this:

6:00 A.M.	Up and dress.
6:30	Fix breakfast for my husband and feed the baby.

7:00	Get older boy up and give him breakfast.
7:45	Leave for class at college, leaving my husband with the children.
9:45	Return home.
10:00	Sit down for coffee with husband.
10:30	Husband leaves for work. His work day is Noon–8:00 P.M. Make beds and pick up.
11:30	Bathe baby and dress her.
Noon	Fix baby's lunch and feed her. Eat lunch myself.
1:00 P.M.	Put baby to bed. Nap.
3:00	Up and start dinner.
3:30	Son comes home from school.
4:00	Help son with homework.
5:00	Set table.
5:15	Eat dinner with children.
6:00	Clean up after dinner, wash children, get children into pajamas, dress for work.
7:00	Pick up babysitter and leave for work.
9:00	Husband returns. (Three nights a week, the sitter gets picked up and taken home. Sometimes Mrs. A.'s husband works very late. When that happens, Mrs. A. takes the sitter home at 2:00 A.M. when she returns from work.)
2:30 A.M.	To bed.

Theresa says the late afternoon–early evening time before she leaves the house is always difficult. Her husband is home when she leaves in the morning, so the kids don't care. But even though it's really only a couple of hours most nights, it's the end of the day and they are tired, and she's usually rushing in order to have dinner ready, eat dinner, clean up, get them ready for the night, and pick up the sitter. She feels she should do all of this, although she admits it would be easier if the sitter took over part. (Black, two-parent.)

Dee is a young lawyer with a ten-month-old infant. Her husband is a lawyer, too. She says her constant worry is that the excellent woman she has working for her five days a week will get sick. It happened one day last week, and the resulting crisis is one that Dee will remember for a long time. "The day started normally. We both got up at 6:00. Jim went to shower and shave. I changed the baby and gave him breakfast. Jim played with him while I showered and began to dress. At 7:00 A.M., Mrs. Jones called to say she'd been up all night with a stomach virus and wouldn't come in. She'd already tried to get a replacement but couldn't. Jim had an important client coming in at 9:30 and had to be at the office. I was due in court that morning on an important case. Jim said if it were any other client, he'd break the appointment, but this man was just too important to the office. It was my first time in court and I knew there was no way I could explain this. I started to call two 'backup' child-care women, but both were busy. I considered calling my office and lying: 'I've just been run over. I'm in the Emergency Room of the Hospital. The doctor thinks I may have an emergency appendectomy.' Finally, I called my mother in the city. She agreed to stay home from her job and I brought the baby to her home in the city on the way to my office. Jim and I talked that night when it was all over. We decided we must have a couple of absolute fallback positions in case of an emergency. After all, things do happen, and you can't always anticipate them. But I guess there are no absolutes and we'll just have to get used to living with more uncertainty." (White, two-parent.)

THE PROBLEMS OF DAILY LIVING: THE SINGLE MOTHER

For single parents, the situation may be even more difficult. Among other problems of the one-parent family is the lack of help at the peak times of household chores and family responsibilities. One young woman said to us that as a result she's always tired. "It's not that Kyla is difficult, she's not. She's a good baby and cute but everything takes time and there's not enough. I get up every weekday morning at 5:30, shower and eat breakfast myself first. At 6:30, I wake up the baby, wash and change her, get her dressed and give her a bath. Then I dress her to go out and walk to my sister's where I leave the baby. She gives her breakfast, too. I get to work by 7:30 and leave at 3:30. I pick up the baby at 4:00 and two times a week, I take her while I market and usually twice a week, we go home first and then I pick up the laundry and go to the laundromat. By 5:30, we're back home and I fix dinner and at 6:30 I feed the baby and I eat, too. Between 7:30 and 8:30, I usually play with the baby and sometimes we both sit and watch TV. Afterwards, I put together the baby's things to take the next day to the sitter and then I bathe the baby, get her ready for bed and put her to bed at 9:00. I set my hair, decide what I'll wear in the morning and go to bed, usually about 10:30." (Black, one-parent.)

Meg is a partner in a management consultant firm in New York. Although her work permits much more daily flexibility than the average job, it is very demanding work and usually requires her to work at home nights and weekends. As a result, Meg tends to get up an hour earlier than the children, so that she can get a quiet early morning hour for work before there are demands on her. On what she describes as a typical day, she got up at 6:00 A.M. and worked on a special report until 7:30. Then she awakened the children, washed and dressed the youngest (age two), left her with the older one (age five), and showered and dressed herself. "I prepared a lunchbox for the five-year-old, changing contents twice in response to special requests. Brushed the five-year-old's hair, checked her appearance, dressed the baby and put both into the car. Dropped the baby at nursery school and the older one at kindergarten. Drove to the station and caught the train for New York, at the office before 10:00 A.M.. Left the office at 5:30 and home by 6:30. The housekeeper works from 3:00 to 7:00 P.M. She picks up the two-year-old at nursery school and the five-year-old from a friend's house where the child goes each day after kindergarten. Then she brings them home, straightens up the house, does the children's laundry and gets dinner ready and bathes the children." When Meg gets home at 6:30, she just about has time to get in and get her coat off when the housekeeper leaves. Meg and the children have dinner. Meg clears away the dishes and puts them in the machine. She puts the baby to bed at 8:00 and then she and the older one play or watch TV for an hour. Then at 9:15 or 9:30, she puts the older girl to bed. "There are usually half a dozen requests for water or another kiss or a forgotten story from the day. It's usually 10 or 10:30 before she goes to sleep. That leaves me about an hour or so to review work for the next day, write myself some notes, get ready for bed." (Black, one-parent.)

The Needs of Working Mothers

After describing how she managed the first year of a psychiatric residency and a household with two preschool-age children, a husband, a large dog, two cats, and one bird, a young physician told us, "Here's my list of the essentials a woman should have if she expects to work full time and be a good wife and mother. Anything less than this means living on a tightrope, and since most of the women I see have much less, each day is another balancing act."

Her list follows:

- plenty of strength and good health
- the capacity to organize and to be well organized yourself, no matter what
- the support and encouragement of a husband
- the active assistance of a husband, relative, or paid help
- acceptance of the fact that some things will not get done, and others will go wrong
- the ability to set priorities and to put children and husband ahead of housework
- seeing the benefits in all this, not just for yourself but for your children, too (Mine have become far more independent and self-reliant since I went back to work.)
- Some time for yourself
- Some vacation time when the whole family can be together and enjoy each other without always feeling hassled about time and undone work

And then she added, laughing: "Of course, it helps if you have a sense of humor, patience, and the disposition of an angel." (Black, two-parent.)

A keypunch operator, who was separated at the time of the interview, would have added near the top of the list, "a sympathetic employer and a job with a flexible routine, or at least some flexibility about beginning and leaving times." (Black, one-parent.)

The Informal Support System: The Importance of Family

Although women frequently mentioned neighbors or friends as providing important help, it is clear from the interviews that the single most important source of help for working mothers are relatives and family. Whether for child-care purposes, emergencies, advice, or just encouragement and sympathy, most of these women view "family" as an essential support system.

The specific sources of help, in the order and frequency mentioned by the women studied were:

- husband
- mother
- other close relatives (sister, father, brother, grandmother, aunt, in-law)
- close friends
- colleagues
- physicians
- mental health professionals*
- ministers

A nursing supervisor was quite specific as she discussed her approach to obtaining help for problems: "If the problem is financial, my husband and I sit down and talk it out. If it's about the baby, I tend to discuss it with my mother first. She's had seven of us and I figure she's experienced. If I have a fight with my husband, I talk to my best friend. The four of us—her husband, mine, Janie, and I—have been friends since high school, so I don't feel I'm exposing Don when I talk. Once in a while, I talk to the ward chief. We've worked together here for ten years, and he's easy to talk to and usually gives good advice." (White, two-parent.)

*We will discuss the use of professionals in providing help later in this chapter.

Apart from the amount of help they get from their husbands, many women stressed the enormous importance of relatives as providing a natural, informal source of support. Although the family as a support system was mentioned by all, it is clearly among blacks and among working-class families of both races that relatives play a particularly significant role. We described earlier (Chapter 3) the extensive role played by relatives in providing child care, either in the child's home or in the relative's home. We discuss here how the women interviewed view their relatives, especially mothers, sisters, and other close relatives as key individuals to go to for help around a variety of problems.

We explored, in particular, the nature and extensiveness of contacts these women had with family members. After all, almost all worked full time. Most commented also on the constant time pressure, indeed a constant sense of never having enough time to manage essentials, let alone time for themselves. "All my time and effort goes into keeping my head above water, just coping on a day-to-day basis." (White, two-parent.)

Similarly, a repeated theme was the lack of time for any kind of social life. Many of the women who returned to work after having been home for a few years expressed a sense of loss with regard to friends. "I wonder if I will ever have the same kind of relationship or if it is just impossible once you are working. We would meet for lunch and go to a museum or sometimes just talk and gossip on the phone. I know it sounds like nonsense, but I really always thought we could rely on one another no matter what happened. Now I rarely phone because I never have time to sit and chat." (White, two-parent, social worker.)

Despite this "pressure cooker" existence—with little time for themselves, not enough time for children and no time for friends, a major finding of our study is the extraordinarily high frequency of contacts these women maintained with extended family—relatives and kin. Perhaps, as several women suggested, the extensiveness and continuity of family relationships may be, at least in part, a consequence of a life-style that requires external support wherever possible, just to keep functioning. Regardless, for some women regular, frequent contacts with relatives are a source of essential concrete help. For others, family means reassurance, intimacy, and support in a crisis.

More specifically, we asked our interviewees how often they saw and spoke to their families. Counting a large family gathering at Thanksgiving Day dinner when fifteen or twenty relatives were present as a single contact only, we asked how many times in the past month these women had seen (visited with) their own family and how often, their husband's family? And we asked the same questions regarding frequency of contact through telephone conversations during the last week. Despite all the conventional talk about the diminished relationship people have with extended family, an extraordinarily high frequency of contacts were maintained, as can be seen in Table 6–1.

Among the working-class families, the frequency of contacts was even higher, especially for the black families, all of whom maintained daily or frequent contact with relatives. The white one-parent families had the smallest number of family contacts among the group studied.

In short, working mothers are in close contact with their extended families. Working-class families and black families generally maintain especially strong family relationships. Whether or not there is something unique about the group of white single mothers in this sample, we would note that if they were indeed characteristic of such women generally, it would suggest one other area of potential stress for the single mother: the absence of a strong, informal family support system.

For these women who have frequent contacts with family members, the family continues to be viewed as central and as an essential support, in particular for working families. Grandmothers, aunts, and great-aunts may no longer live in the home with many of our families, but they are accessible, available, and supportive for most of these young women. For example:

Jane is a registered nurse who works from 7:30 A.M. to 3:30 P.M. Her husband is a full-time graduate student working for his master's degree in business administration. They have two children, a one-year-old and a four-year-old. A day she described as fairly typical goes something like this:

5:00 A.M.	Get up, shower, brush teeth.
5:30	Make coffee; prepare baby's breakfast.
5:45	Dress.

TABLE 6-1. Frequency of Contacts with Relatives[a]

	Daily Visits and Telephone Calls	Daily Visits	Daily Telephone Calls	Frequent Visits[b]	Occasional Visits[c]	Rare Visits[d]	No Contact
Two-Parent, Professional Families							
White (45)	3	8	8[e]	20	6	6	1
Black (30)	2	4	2	16	3	3	2
Two-Parent, Working-Class Families							
White (30)	2	12	5	14	1	—	—
Black (38)	8	20	10	10	—	—	—
One-Parent, Professional and Working-Class Families							
White, Professional (7)	—	2	—	1	1	1	2
White, Working-Class (23)	—	6	—	9	2	3	3
Black, Professional (5)	—	2	—	3	—	—	—
Black, Working-Class (26)	—	16	4	6	—	—	2

[a]Excluding relatives who lived in same household as the women.
[b]More than one visit per week in the past month.
[c]More than once in the past month but less than once a week.
[d]Only one time in the past month.
[e]All except one woman was in daily phone contact with one relative and also had frequent or occasional visits with others during the past month, thus the total is more than forty-five.

111

6:15	Change, dress, and feed baby.
6:45	Leave for work, bringing baby to sister's along the way.
7:00	Husband awakens four-year-old and helps him get washed and dressed.
7:30	Husband prepares breakfast for son and himself, and they eat together.
8:15	Husband and son put on heavy jackets and walk to school.
Noon	Husband picks up son at school and brings him to sister's house and then leaves for school.
4:00 P.M.	Arrive home from work and go to get children. Visit with sister for a half-hour or so.
5:00	Play with children.
5:45	Prepare dinner.
6:15	Feed baby.
6:45	Dinner for husband, self, and four-year-old.
7:15	Make lunches for next day while husband cleans up.
7:45	Baby gotten ready for bed. Parents play with baby.
8:00	Husband puts baby to bed.
8:30	Put older child to bed.
9:00	Parents have coffee and relax.
10:00	In bed.

Donna T. works as a medical secretary in a local hospital. She has two daughters, Kim, ten months old, and Sharon, four and a half. Donna's work day is 8:00 A.M.–5:00 P.M. She is married, and her husband is a salesman. A typical day for Donna is something like this:

6:00 A.M.	Out of bed and shower.
6:15	Wake up baby, wash and dress her and wake up Sharon.
6:30	Give baby breakfast.
6:45	Put baby in crib and prepare Sharon's breakfast.
7:00	Get dressed.
7:15	Collect baby's clothes for sitter; check Sharon.
7:20	Leave house.
7:25	Drop baby off at sitter's.
7:30	Take Sharon to mother's (grandmother's).

8:00	Begin work.
8:30	(Grandfather takes Sharon to school when he leaves for work.)
5:00 P.M.	Leave work.
5:15	Catch bus for home.
5:40	Get off bus into car to pick up children.
5:45	Reach parents' house to get Sharon. Visit.
6:30	Arrive home and start to prepare dinner. (Husband already home.)
7:00	Dinner.
7:30	Dishes (done together).
7:45	Play with children.
8:00	Get baby ready for bed.
8:15	Bathe Sharon while husband puts baby to bed.
8:30	Husband plays with Sharon. Straighten the house, do some laundry.
9:00	Sharon to bed (either parent).
9:30	Prepare baby's clothes and bottle for next day, finish laundry.
10:00	Watch TV with husband; talk.
11:30	To bed.

In describing this day, Donna commented, "Of course, it was an easier day than usual. My husband had a different assignment this month. Usually, he works late three nights a week, which means he's not around to help. And then, I wouldn't have the use of the car after work to pick up the children from my parents' home. I would have to walk from the bus stop, which is ten blocks from their home, and then either my brother would drive me home or I call a taxi." She added, "Since I had the car, I could stay longer with my parents, too. It gave me a chance to talk to my mother for a while. She's making some clothes for Sharon and wanted me to see them."

Weekends, too, offer obvious opportunity for frequent family contacts. The ritual of Sunday dinner may have disappeared in many families, but weekly or biweekly visits to grandparents remain a part of the routine in many families. In others, a more informal, casual "dropping in" to visit a married sister or brother-in-law is a frequent part of family life. For many of the women we interviewed, "living near the family" was an important criterion in deciding where they lived.

Family as the Focus of Daily Life

In addition to stressing the importance of relatives in providing a variety of help and support, most of the women emphasized how central a role their own immediate family played in their lives. As part of this "family-centeredness," working mothers and working parents seem to spend an extraordinary amount of time with their children during weekends and all available holidays. Several women discussed their attitudes toward child time and family time, saying that almost all the time they had at home went toward being with their children. "Since we both work, the weekends are strictly for the family. We may go out or visit or do something, but we do it all together. It would never occur to us to do something without the children." (White, two-parent, working-class.)

"From the time I come home until the time she [daughter, aged two and a half] goes to bed, and all weekend long, she's with me constantly." (Black, one-parent.)

"It's not the quantity of time spent with a child that matters; it's the quality. When I was home all the time, I was bored and irritable. I would sit around and watch TV or call a friend and talk. I was home but I didn't do anything special with the baby. Since I went back to work, it's very different. When I leave work, I look forward to picking up Alison at the day care center. We take the bus home together and she tells me about her day and I tell her little things about mine. She helps me set the table at night and we do things together and we both enjoy it. It's much better now for both of us." (White, one-parent, working-class.)

"With me working, the kids get less time from me, but more from my husband. And whatever time they get from me is all theirs," said a social worker who had recently returned to work after being at home for almost three years. "Working mothers have less time to spend with their children, but the time that is available is fully concentrated on the child—and on enjoying the child." (White, two-parent.)

"The real difference is that now my husband spends time with the boy. It's not that he didn't spend time with him before, but it's different now," said a woman who had just gotten a job as a data clerk when her son entered a preschool program last month. "He [my husband] would play with the boy, sometimes, but not much else. Now my husband picks him up at my mother's on his way home. And while I get supper ready, he gets the boy into his pajamas and then we eat together and he plays with him and usually puts him to bed. The boy loves it and I think my husband enjoys it too, even though he says he does it only to help me, since I can't manage everything when I come home at night." (Black, two-parent, working-class.)

On the other hand, as several women reminded us, when both parents, or the sole parent, work full time and have children, there's not much time left for anything else. "That means something has got to go, and that something is usually friends—or any kind of social life. I guess we live like hermits. Sometimes I miss seeing friends, but I think most of them are in the same boat as we are. They don't have any more time to socialize than we do. Maybe it gets easier when the kids are older, but I'm not sure."[1] (White, two-parent.)

Thus, the daily home and family life of the women in our study is clearly centered on "family"—their own immediate families and their and their husband's families and relatives. The family is the focus of daily living, and "family" in the larger sense is a source of essential help and support, whether concrete and practical or reassuring and nurturing. Friends and neighbors may be viewed as important, too, but the role they play is much less significant than that of relatives, at least for the women we interviewed.

The Formal Support System

Clearly, it is the natural informal support system—the family and to a much smaller extent friends and neighbors—which provides the bulk of support to our working mothers. Yet despite this, we found that the formal support system does play a significant role in providing needed help.

Community resources were used by most of the women at some time or another; however, few were mentioned as particularly helpful. In part because most of the women had preschool-age children only, they were unfamiliar with many of the services which might exist, since their needs were largely focused on home and young children. Their interest in formal, organized services were concentrated in these areas. Several women mentioned a health clinic or a physician who maintained evening or weekend hours; however, apart from some disparate individual responses, it seemed overwhelmingly clear that there is only one formal resource that assumes any real importance for these women, and that is some form of child-care program.

Just as child care looms as the most important concern of working mothers, child-care programs—day care centers, family day care homes, preschool programs—are the single most important community resource as far as these women are concerned.

It is in this context, therefore, that when we explored what these women considered to be the major gaps in community service provisions, almost all had to do with inadequacies related to child care.

Among the most frequently mentioned specific lacks in the formal "support" system are:

- inadequate numbers of child-care programs, in particular, preschool programs with reasonable income-related fees
- too short a day in prekindergarten and kindergarten programs and often uncoordinated schedules which made it especially difficult for families with two or more children.
- too rigid school hours ("Why not open one hour earlier and close one or two hours later? It would make such a difference to working parents.")
- inadequate numbers of after-school programs for preschool and primary school–age children
- nonexistent cafeteria or school lunch programs in primary school
- inadequate or nonexistent local public transportation
- no easily accessible information and referral service for

families wanting information about family day care mothers, emergency caregivers, reliable casual baby sitting—in addition to group programs
- inadequate summer facilities and activities for children when schools are closed

Other needs, mentioned by a much smaller number of women, included: flexitime (flexible starting and ending times at work); more shared jobs or part-time work; infant day care and programs for toddlers; more flexible store hours; availability of repair services outside of the standard work day and work week; opening schools for children from the age of three; family life and parent education programs; "a service that sends nurses to the homes of families with new children and teaches parents good infant care and examines the babies."

Apart from child care and other child-related services, the only other formal support program mentioned by a significant number of women was some sort of individual or family counseling service. About 20 percent of the sample were currently seeing a mental health professional. We include in this group of professionals the individual psychiatrists, psychologists, and social workers which some women identified as providing some kind of psychotherapeutic help, as well as the family service agencies or community mental health services that other women specified as a source of similar information, advice, and guidance. Among all the women we interviewed, the white single mothers were the group most likely to be seeking professional help. They explained to us that they sought such help either to learn how to cope with complicated lives alone or to learn how to manage stressful intra-family relationships for a child caught between two parents—or abandoned by one parent, the father. Often the child's problems became visible only as they surfaced in a group or school situation and the mother saw the consequences outside of the family. For some women, professional help was sought to help a child in difficulty. A few others said that under certain circumstances, they might seek professional counseling but they had not yet done so and did not plan to within the immediate future. One woman in the study suffered an emotional breakdown which required hospitalization shortly before the second interview.

Perhaps we should note here that none of the women who were receiving any form of psychotherapy or related help indicated that the problem for which they sought help had to do with their working-mother role. As we indicated, several women found it difficult coping with the "single mother" role. Our impression is that although the time and task pressures might be greater for single women than married women, work and a job made it easier for these women to cope with the emotional strain, in particular their social isolation. Among the married women who sought help, the most frequent reason given had to do with marital problems; of lesser importance were child-related problems. None of the women mentioned difficulties at work, difficulties in coping with the work, family pressures, or even guilt regarding less time spent with children as a reason for seeking help.

Thus, although these various mental health services were described as useful by a number of women, we would guess that their value was not greater for working mothers than for nonworking mothers.

In contrast, the formal child-care and child-related services mentioned earlier clearly represent a significant contribution toward meeting the special needs of working mothers. Indeed, such programs were mentioned repeatedly as being essential components of a formal support system, and the major criticism of Maplewood is the extent to which these women found these key services unavailable, inaccessible, or nonexistent.

Regardless, we would emphasize that when we asked these women to tell us what they viewed as the *most important needs of working mothers* in addition to *child-care arrangements*, the listing tended to minimize formal supports and emphasize more the informal natural support systems as well as personal resources, discussed earlier.

Summary

Although most women acknowledge the complex and stressful nature of their daily lives, few think of themselves as having an especially hard life, or even as having any particular personal problems as a consequence. There are practical problems, but most will disappear in time. At least that is how most women view their condition.

They see the needs of working mothers as including a variety of practical concrete child-care services, programs, and activities, depending on the age of their child or children. Other than that, they view themselves as needing—or using—few formal community resources.

Apart from the critical need for good child-care arrangements, which for some, especially those with very young children, still means informal child care, women include as essentials the help and support of husbands and other family members, wherever possible. Women who can, use paid help, but most see this as an unlikely resource in their own families. Others hope for greater assistance from husbands within the home and help and support from other relatives outside the home.

The informal, natural support system is essential for these women, and at its core is the help provided by relatives. Two families moved to be closer to relatives. Others mentioned this as a reason for choosing their current place of residence. Family members in the sense of relatives and kinfolk—grandparents, siblings, in-laws—provide essential concrete help in the way of child care, and, perhaps equally important, they offer reassurance, advice, information, support, and practical help of a variety of types. For these working mothers, the family continues to be the single most important institution in their lives and in the lives of their husbands and children.

Note

1. For a discussion of how dual-career couples find that a social life and friendships are what go by the wayside in families trying to maintain two careers and parenting, see Rhona Rapoport and Robert Rapoport, *Dual Career Families* (London: Penguin, 1971).

7

Toward a Policy and Program Agenda for Working Parents

What We Learned from the Study

The most significant social phenomenon in the industrial societies of the mid-twentieth century is the large-scale entry of women into the labor force, in particular the accelerated labor force participation rate of young married women with preschool children. This development is generating a social revolution in family life-styles in the United States. Almost half of husband-wife families have two wage-earners; 60 percent of the women of childbearing age are in the work force; and by the end of the 1980s this group is likely to increase to 70 percent. Seventy percent of the working women hold jobs because of economic necessity, and with continued inflation this percentage is likely to increase. Furthermore, a significant additional percentage work for compelling family economic reasons, if not out of absolute necessity.

Two hundred women, half of them white, half of them black, and all with at least one preschool-age child, were interviewed in order to obtain insights and new information on how these women are coping with this life-style, which is increasingly emerging as the modal life-style for American families—as for most other families living in advanced Western industrial countries. The women interviewed were either continuing work after the birth of a child or reentering the labor market some years after a child's birth. Two-thirds of the women were married and living with their husbands; the remaining third were single mothers and the sole wage-earners in their families. Approximately half of the women can be described as professionals, middle-level managers or executives; the other half as office workers, blue-collar workers, or paraprofessionals. A significant number of single mothers in transition from public assistance to earned income only were also involved in the study. The women were interviewed twice, once at the point of the major life-style transition (childbirth; returning to the labor force as a parent) and then a second time six months later to review the adjustment and adaptation process.

Despite the rhetoric in the United States that emphasizes concern for children and families, the reality which surfaces in this study of women trying to cope with both family and work lives suggests very little sensitive response. It seems clear that our world is not set up to make it easy to manage home, children, and work simultaneously.

Child care is by far the most important problem these women have to contend with. Neither the problem of child care nor the solutions are very different among professional or nonprofessional women, middle- or low-income mothers, regardless of race or family structure. The most significant factor in determining the type of child care used—and preferred—by working mothers is the age of their child. School—preschool, nursery school, prekindergarten, kindergarten—is the single most important child-care mode for children aged three to five, just as it is for children of this age nationally. Regardless of its prevalence and popularity, however, it is rarely the sole care mode, primarily because preschool is often a short day or at most a normal school day, and this does not cover the full working day for mothers. For this reason, as well as certain others mentioned below, child care for the children of working mothers can best be described as a "package" involving elements such as kindergarten, day care, family day care, a spouse, a relative's home, or a teenage babysitter. More than half of the preschool children experience two or more forms of child care during a routine week. Children aged three, four, or five are particularly likely to experience multiple forms of child care. Moreover, over 25 percent of the families coordinate a complicated multimode child-care package, since the presence of two or more children substantially increases the likelihood of requiring multiple child-care arrangements. Inevitably, the tensions attendant on keeping the system functioning are ever present for these women.

The greatest diversity is found in types of child care used for infants and toddlers (children under the age of three). White professional two-parent families are likely to use in-home, paid child care. Working-class two-parent families are likely to share child care between parents who work different shifts, use some form of relative care either in their own homes or in the home of the relative, or use family day care. One-parent families are most likely to use a day care center, either because they prefer such care or because they are more likely to be eligible for subsidized care, which is more available in centers.

There is extensive use of relatives in providing child care for at least some portion of the time care is needed, and husbands play an important role in two-parent families.

Child-care needs and problems continue to weigh heavily on working mothers. Nor does there seem to be any easing of the situation in sight. There is a shortage of subsidized group programs—both preschool programs for three- to five-year-olds and infant and toddler child-care programs. Many preschools are part-day, and almost all kindergartens are, which creates additional problems for mothers who may have had a three- or four-year-old in a full-day nursery school and now, at five, this child is suddenly experiencing a shorter day. Many suburban schools refuse to permit children who live within a mile of the school to have lunch at school, and other schools still do not provide a

school lunch or permit any child to remain at school at lunchtime! Few schools provide programs for children during the short
or long school vacations.

There is little in the way of infant and toddler child-care programs for those who are interested in using such programs. Moreover, little reliable information is available to parents regarding
family day care mothers, or, equally important, competent
women who can take over in an emergency if a regular caregiver
is ill or if a child is ill and cannot attend his/her usual program or
school that day.

A significant amount of child care is informal and free, or at
least nonmonetized. Much of the informal monetized care is
quasi-market and, therefore, still low-cost. A relatively small
amount of child care is paid for at full market value.

Although modified traditional gender roles continue to domi-
nate in the allocation of most household tasks, a majority of the
women interviewed described some movement toward greater
equity in fulfilling household responsibilities. In particular, they
stressed more sharing than was true in their parental households
or in their own families before they worked or before the birth of
their child. Furthermore, regardless of who has responsibility for
these chores, and how much is done by the woman, these women
stressed equity between spouses as a central value in marriage,
even though the reality may still be very different. No one likes to
relinquish power, but it would seem that men are realizing that
when a woman contributes substantially to the family's income,
she is entitled to some help along the way. A major finding of the
study is that when there is a sense of equity in the sharing of tasks
women describe their marriage and households as much happier
than otherwise.

Although "family" continues to be primary in the lives of
these women, "work" plays an increasingly important role in
their lives, too. Most of the women interviewed expect to work
all their adult lives, just as most adult men do. Although clearly
the overwhelming majority state that they are working for economic reasons, most also say that they would continue to work
even if there were no longer any financial need. Professional
women stress the importance of careers or work as a central

source of personal gratifications. Single mothers emphasize the role of work as the basis of social relationships and supplementary life experiences. Only among the two-parent working-class families do a majority of the women say they would stop working if the family no longer needed their earnings. And even within this group half of those indicated that, if part-time work were available, they would take such employment in order to continue obtaining the personal satisfaction that work can provide while alleviating the pressure on family life coming from full-time employment.

Thus, child-care problems are a source of constant stress and are only partially solved by existing resources. Intrafamily household and home problems are just beginning to respond to some increased role equity within the family. Purchased services are far outside the reach of most families, but husband's help and the help of other relatives attenuate some of the strain. In contrast, there has been almost no adaptation on the part of the work place. As a consequence, work pressures continue to impinge severely on parenting and family-related needs and conditions.

Neither statutory provisions nor employment-related fringe benefits provide much in the way of parent-related benefits. Very few of these women—or women in the country generally—possess any real entitlements to maternity benefits and leaves, and none have any right to a sickness benefit related to caring for an ill child at home. Although some women use their own sickness and vacation benefits to cover maternity or other child-related needs, this is implemented on an informal basis at best and sometimes is done sub rosa. As a consequence, those women who continued work after childbirth took off an average of six weeks after childbirth, half of the minimum statutory entitlement of almost all other industrialized countries and one-quarter of what is becoming the standard benefit in Northern Europe. Although some women returned quickly to work because of career pressures, the majority of those who took off a very short time after birth did so because of intense economic needs.

In addition to the obvious lack of child-parenting and family-related benefits at work, employers continue to be unsympathetic and often downright hostile to mothers at the work place.

The women report that in applying for jobs they encounter employers of an older generation (with at-home wives) who quiz them on their plans for taking care of their children. These questions are illegal, but they are still asked. Employers create an inevitable double bind for working mothers. They provide no benefits to facilitate women's coping with parenting responsibilities. Yet if women make such a request, this is used to underscore the "secondary" nature of women's employment and their lack of serious commitment to a job and the labor market generally.

We mentioned earlier that although the supply of child-care services at reasonable cost continues to be inadequate, the choice of child-care mode is more a factor of the child's age than anything else and that only for younger children do class, race, and family structure influence choice around such issues as the use of paid in-home care, relative care, or out-of-home care, respectively. Clearly, family structure influences the patterns of how household responsibilities are fulfilled, since by definition there is rarely any person to share tasks within a one-parent family. Even if there is no assurance of sharing in a two-parent family, a far greater possibility for sharing does exist. In constrast, neither race, class, nor family structure influence the extent of work-related problems and pressures. Furthermore, although the type of job does affect the extent and intensity of work–family strain, it is more a question of specific jobs rather than a distinction between professional and less skilled occupations. Thus, low-skilled work such as family day care or teacher aide may lead to less strain between home and work. The same is true for teaching generally and for work done at home (e.g., a practicing psychotherapist whose office is at home, a freelance writer.) On the other hand, for many professionals, work is a seven-day-a-week occupation, including many evenings as well. Thus, some combination of specific jobs, occupations which permit autonomy and flexibility, and individual personality may be the determining factors in attenuating work–family stress, given the current unresponsiveness of the work situation for most employees.

In analyzing the pattern of needs, problems, and solutions of working mothers across race, class, and family structure, we were struck most by the significance of family structure and less by race and class, except as exacerbating factors. For example: The major problems faced by the black families when compared to the white families are lower income and less job satisfaction. Although clearly of major importance, neither of these is unique to black working mothers. Indeed, the black two-parent families had incomes well above national and state median income levels, because two earners make a difference in all families. The significant differences in family income are more a factor of male wage differentials, higher unemployment rates, or high rates of female-headed families. On the other hand, the black working-class families and one-parent families are far more likely to have extensive informal supports available to them. These families see more of their relatives and make greater use of them in providing child care as well as a variety of other forms of help and reassurance.

The major difference between the professional and working-class families is primarily one of income and attitude toward work. Clearly, the financial rewards of work are greater for the professional families. In part, this leads to a greater use in purchased services, in contrast to working-class families whose major source of help is nonmonetized—through relatives, friends, or neighbors. However, this does not mean that either type of service is by definition better service. Furthermore, although their attitude toward work may be expressed in different ways, work plays a significant role in the values and sense of personal worth of all these women regardless of class.

The most significant differences in the problems of the working mothers in our study are primarily related to family structure and, to a much lesser extent, to marital satisfaction in our two-parent families. For all the women in our study, managing child care, household tasks and responsibilities, and job-related pressures presents a constant strain—a combination of time and energy pressures that often seems almost insurmountable. Most of the families described—and the women we interviewed—seem to be coping with a stressful life-style with incredible ingenuity and creativity. Their solutions are tenuous and complicated and often acceptable only because they are clearly transitory. Many women maintain an attitude like that of the mother who said, "Prob-

lems? Problems? Who has time for problems?" At best the situation is difficult, and the women are astonishing in their capacity
to cope with relative equanimity.

But for some the situation is particularly bad. For the married woman whose husband continues to assume a traditional
male role in the home, expecting his wife to fulfill all household
responsibilities despite a full-time job outside the home, the situation is very tough. We looked at some women's time budgets
and wondered: How could they manage an eight-hour work day,
one hour or more of travel time to and from work, and six hours
every weekday of child and household responsibilities in addition
to full-time child care on weekends? If their husbands were am-
bivalent about their working—let alone opposed to it—this created major problems. Indeed, two wives in family situations such
as this separated from their husbands during the course of our
study. However, these extreme family situations were in the minority for two-parent families.

In contrast, almost all our single mothers lived under constant time and energy pressures, and most had to contend with
economic strain too. Obviously, the major difference between
our one- and two-parent families is economic. Family income is
significantly reduced when there is only one wage-earner in a
family, and the reduction is even more marked when the sole
wage-earner is a woman. However, the problems of occupational segregation, job training, and wage equity, although of great
importance, would be significant whether these women were
mothers or not. The problem of inadequate family income when
children are present is, however, of great significance, and will
be discussed again later in this chapter.

For the most part, two-parent families can be assured of two
sources of income. In addition, these families have four hands
and two persons available for tasks instead of two hands and one
person. Thus they share tasks, expand time availability, permit
the division of responsibilities and the alleviation of emotional
stress and strain. They even have the potential of two sources of
informal supports in the form of a double set of relatives.

In contrast, single mothers have less of almost everything, except, perhaps, problems. They are, of course, saved the possible
additional load of a husband's problems at the same time as they

are deprived of all such possible help. In addition to the probability of less income, single working mothers have at their disposal less time, less energy, fewer skills, and less support both in and out of the home.

If a marriage is bad, these women find their single status relieves them of the additional strain of fighting, conflict, tension—and often of husbands who gave no help anyway. But coping with child care, childrearing, home responsibilities, and work pressures when you are alone is very difficult. And most of these women have no options. They must work. Hearing them describe how they managed their homes, their jobs, and their children (often in isolation and loneliness) was painful and poignant. Their daily lives often seemed incredibly difficult, and they received little support anywhere.

In essence, for all of these women and their families, it seems quite clear: Being a member of the labor force and a full-time parent means trying to manage against overwhelming odds in an unresponsive society.

Implications for a Policy and Program Agenda

Nothing we would say here is original or unique. Our focus is clearly on the needs of wage-earning adults who also happen to be parents, on working mothers when they are the sole parent, and on working mothers and fathers when both parents in a two-parent family are employed. As stated earlier, we are not here addressing broader social policy issues, which require attention regardless of whether the adults are parents or not. Thus, the income, employment, and training needs of blacks in general or women regardless of race require attention with or without the presence of children.

However, the income needs of families with young children—and of adults rearing children—clearly are of particular significance as we identify the problems of working parents.

Women who are sole parents are likely to suffer major financial hardships with consequences for their children.[1] Thirty-six percent of all female-headed families in the United States had incomes below the poverty level in 1977. Although female-headed families constitute 15 percent of the total number of families in the United States, they represent over half of the families living in poverty. Moreover, more than half of the 10 million children living in families with incomes below the poverty level were in one-parent families. In 1977, 861,000 families of the 8.2 million families headed by women had only one source of income—public assistance—and almost all of them were living below the poverty level. Of the 675,000 families headed by women that had earnings and also received public assistance, over 61 percent were below the poverty level. Among families with children, the median income of $6,358 for families headed by women was only one-third of the median income of husband-wife families.

Regardless of what else is done to improve the wage-earning capacities of women, it is time to address the low-income status of female-headed families even when the women are in the labor force and work full time. For these families, as well as for the other 5 million children in families with an employed father and income below the poverty level, surely it is time to provide a child or family allowance—a cash benefit provided to families based on the presence and number of minor children in the family. The United States is the only one of sixty-five industrialized countries that does not provide such a benefit—which would assure a direct cash income supplement to all families with children. Although the benefit provided in other countries varies in size, even a small amount can help in a family with very low income. This benefit can be provided as a direct cash transfer or indirectly, as a refundable tax credit.

The recently expanded earned income tax credit in the United States represents a variation on this approach for low-income working parents. But we would urge the need now to develop some form of income transfer for all families with children, not just families with working mothers, even if the policy were to make such a benefit taxable.

In contrast, one way to provide an income support benefit specific to working mothers would be to offer a paid maternity or parental leave for employed women (or perhaps a benefit to be shared between employed husbands and wives). Such a policy, assuring wage replacement and full job protection for a specified period of time following childbirth, would be of enormous importance in protecting income for families dependent on two wages or on the sole wage of a mother. In addition, women would be assured that their jobs would be held for them, and that they would not risk unemployment if they remained home for some weeks after childbirth. Recently passed legislation in the United States provides such benefits only to women covered under private disability insurance. Approximately 40 percent of the working women in the United States have such coverage as a result. (A much smaller percentage were covered among the women interviewed.)

At present, in Europe, three months is the minimum paid leave provided under law for all employed women. The average leave in the Northern and Eastern European countries is six months, and Sweden provides nine months. Moreover, Sweden and Norway provide for fathers under their legislation through a kind of "parent insurance."

Similarly, neither as a part of federal nor state legislation nor even as part of labor union negotiations has there been an interest expressed in assuring parents a specified number of days of paid sick leave to cover caring for an ill child at home. This too is an employment benefit that is emerging increasingly in several European countries and would be of help to working parents here.

Child care continues to be the central problem for all employed mothers. Our own analyses of national census data suggest that close to 60 percent of the three- to five-year-olds attend some form of out-of-home group programs.[2] Another recent report on child-care arrangements in the United States reports similar figures.[3] Our Maplewood families report the same trend and, perhaps even more important, stress the preference of parents for preschool programs. Parents are clearly using this type of care for three- to five-year-olds. The problem is that most of it is market care and thus inaccessible to a significant portion of the working-class and middle-class families who cannot afford to pay the full market costs of a high-quality preschool program. Of equal importance, however, is the finding that these children are particularly likely to be cared for in multiple arrangements during the week—because many of the preschool programs are part-day, not even as long as the normal school day. At the very least, it should be possible to expand the availability of publicly subsidized preschool progams to make them available to any child of this age whose parents wish him or her to participate.

Furthermore, for these children in preschool and for children aged six to eight in primary schools whose two parents or single parents work, the problem of supplementary school care is crucial also. Parents may need to leave for work before the child leaves for school and return home after school closes, or cope with child care on days that school is closed and the work place is open. We have no data in the United States which indicate how primary school children are cared for now when their parents' work day does not coincide with the normal school day. We need to learn how parents are coping now, and we need to begin to identify different models for supplementary school programs. There are simple things that could be done to make life easier for working families. For example, all schools could provide lunch; schools could open one hour earlier and stay open one or two hours longer, with informal recreational activities available for children who wish to participate. Schools could lower their age of entry and develop a preschool program. The supplementary programs could be administered and operated separately from the regular school program. These are just a few of the possibilities that could be instituted to respond to the changing life-styles of American families.

Finally, with regard to child care, we need to expand the options for infant and toddler care.[4] We are only now beginning to learn about such care; and we are only now beginning to recognize the growing demand for this care. If paid maternity leave were available for some portion of the first year after a child was born, our major concern would be for children from about six months or one year of age to two and a half or so. Parental preferences are not yet clear for child care of children of this age, but it seems highly likely that a variety of types of care will be used and should be available. This suggests the need to expand group care but also to improve the quality of family day care for parents who prefer more informal care. Of particular importance, however, would be some expansion in child-care information and referral services, since many parents say they have great difficulty learning about reliable family day care providers.

Apart from child care, little mention is made of other formal resources as significant family supports. In contrast, great stress is placed on the need for more flexibility and responsiveness at the work place. Flexitime, part-time employment, and shared jobs were mentioned by many as offering possible relief from work/family pressures. Any efforts in this direction should be encouraged.

Our study has highlighted the problems of the single mother. Inadequate income, although central, is only one facet of the problem. It seems clear, also, that work—a job—is essential for these women, not only for obvious economic reasons but for nonpecuniary reasons as well. Work offers a potential source of gratification and often the only source of social contact and relationships in what is frequently a lonely and isolated life. Adequate child-care arrangements become even more important when work is central to both economic and noneconomic needs. In addition, however, single mothers suffer from a lack of time and a lack of physical and emotional support. There is only one person to do all the routine family and household tasks. Friends, neighbors and relatives help, but at best this help is limited, and unless relationships already exist and are very strong these single mothers have little time to cultivate new realtionships. Community agencies interested in responding to the needs of single mothers would do well to experiment with a range of different types of programs, including innovative approaches to providing brief supplementary child care, occasional home-help or other concrete services, information and advice services, and the development of self-help networks.

The recommendations made thus far stem directly from the findings of our study. The women interviewed were clear about the problems and tensions they experienced as part of their daily lives and what would really make a difference—and would really be of help. We would summarize now the questions our study did not answer or those that emerged in the course of the study itself and we would hope to see explored in further work. One ma-

jor regret at the end of the study is that we did not have a budget
that would have permitted systematic interviewing of fathers
(husbands, cohabitants). A few were interviewed informally, because they were present at the time of the scheduled interview,
or because they expressed a special interest. Any subsequent at-
tempt at exploring the family and work lives of working families
should include both parents in order to obtain a more complete
picture of what daily life is like and the extent to which father's
and mother's views of daily routines, problems, and needs do—
or do not—coincide.[5]

The descriptions many of the Maplewood women gave their
average or "typical" days—the complicated arrangements, the
multiplicity of responsibilities, the constant juggling of time and
tasks—underscored how little we know about what Urie Bronfenbrenner has referred to as the natural ecology of children. As
important as data on sickness or health, behavior or misbehavior
may be for quantitative measures of growth, learning, and understanding what is happening to children in our society, we also
need to learn more about the actual daily lives of children, as
they experience their life. We would urge more ethnographic
studies of parenting and childrearing within the home environment in order to provide data about families in real life situations.[6] Similarly, we would urge more use of time studies with
working families.[7] Our own efforts in this study convinced us of
the difficulties in obtaining valid and reliable time-use data.
Time is used in multiple ways simultaneously, and there are
consequent problems in allocating time segments to discrete
tasks. "The laundry is put into the machine and while the wash is
done I get dinner ready. The four-year-old likes to help so she
puts the plates and silver on the table. The baby is in the high
chair and we sing songs and play together. Sometimes I give the
baby supper then." How are we to allocate this half-hour? Yet
despite the difficulty we need to know more about how working
parents use their time. In particular, we should be trying to monitor any increase in the amount of time men invest in household
and family tasks and whether some of the overload is being removed from women. We might hypothesize increasing problems
in those families in which women continue to maintain full
responsibility for home and family even though they are also full-

time workers. We might also hypothesize some positive consequences of an increased involvement in "fathering" or "parenting" roles by men.

In conclusion, we would remind our readers that in their interviews and in their reports on their daily lives, these Maplewood women emphasized once more the centrality and significance of families. Much rhetoric is directed at the value of the family in our society, but little real attention is paid it. For these women, their families—their husbands and children first, and then other family members—are the most important part of their lives. Their jobs, whatever they may be, are a significant part too, but in no way supersede their family relationships. They are trying in every way possible to cope with complicated and demanding routines in order to satisfy what they view as essential responsibilities and obligations in both domains. If their family responsibilities constrain what they can do in the world of work, their families also offer them support which permits them to cope with both worlds. In contrast, however, the world of work continues to impinge on family and home life. As women move increasingly into the work place, both women and men will become more aware of the difficulties in coping with these two domains, unless some modification and adaptation occur.[8] Family life-styles are changing and adapting. Male and female relationships are changing and adapting. If men and women are to become productive adults at home and work—if they are to be parents as well as workers and wage-earners—society too must respond more actively to these changes. In short, there is a policy agenda. Given what is happening to families in our society today, it is time now to respond.

Notes

1. See Beverly L. Johnson, "Women Who Head Families, 1970–1977: Their Numbers Rose, Income Lagged," *Monthly Labor Review*, February 1978. See also Heather L. Ross and Isabell V. Sawhill, *Time of Transition: The Growth of Families Headed by Women* (Washington, D.C.: The Urban In-

stitute, 1975); Clarie Vickery, "Economics and the Single Mother Family," *Public Welfare*, Vol. 36, No. 1 (Winter 1978), and "The Changing Household: Implications for Devising an Income Support Program," *Public Policy*, Vol. XXVI, No. 1 (Winter 1978).

2. Sheila B. Kamerman and Alfred J. Kahn, "Day Care: A Wider View," *The Public Interest* (Winter 1979).

3. Mary Jo Bane *et al.*, "Child Care Arrangements of Working Parents," *Monthly Labor Review*, Vol. 102, No. 10 (October 1979).

4. For an overview of child-care policy for the very young children of employed parents in five European countries, see Sheila B. Kamerman, "Work and Family Life in Industrialized Countries," *SIGNS: The Journal of Women in Culture and Society* (Summer, 1979). For an extensive discussion of these policies and related programs, see Sheila B. Kamerman and Alfred J. Kahn, *Child Care, Family Benefits and Working Parents* (New York: Columbia University Press, 1980).

5. The Working Family Project and the Families and Community Project, at the Wellesley College Center for Research on Women, Laura Lein, Principal Investigator, is one illustration of a study employing such an approach.

6. The current research of Urie Bronfenbrenner involves such an approach.

7. Joseph H. Pleck, Associate Director, Center for the Family, University of Massachusetts, is involved in such an effort now, as is Elliott A. Medrich, Director, Children's Time Study, University of California, Berkeley.

8. For some discussion of this issue, see Kamerman, "Work and Family Life in Industrialized Societies," and Kamerman and Kahn, *Child Care, Family Benefits and Working Parents*.

EPILOGUE

What Do Other Countries Do?*

THIS HAS BEEN the report of a study of what is now the dominant family life-style in the United States—families in which two parents or a sole parent are in the labor force, trying to manage both home and job responsibilities simultaneously—in other words, families with working mothers. As we have indicated, the pattern is now emerging, or has already emerged, as dominant in most of the industrialized world; and it is likely to become so too, in time, in those less industrialized countries in which traditional family styles still predominate. Indeed, almost all the non-Mediterranean European countries have experienced—or are now experiencing—the same revolution as a consequence of the large-scale entry of women into the labor force.

As in the United States, the initial definition of the phenomenon had to do with the changing roles of women—in particular married women—and the consequences for children and fami-

---

*This chapter is based on material gathered as part of a six-country study of child-care policies and programs. The research study was directed jointly by the author and Alfred J. Kahn, co-directors of the Cross-National Research Studies Program at Columbia University School of Social Work. The study was funded by the German Marshall Fund of the United States.

lies. Increasingly, however, the problem has been redefined in these countries and the concerns broadened. Thus, during the 1970s this "women's and children's issue" was viewed as a problem of the changing roles of men and women. Now, as we enter the decade of the 1980s, it seems clear that the concern will be a still broader one, namely, the nature of the relationship between work and family life.

Tension between work and family life is not a new phenomenon. Indeed, it has been noted for some time, and studied and discussed. However, the consequences for family life became more visible when most of the women carrying family responsibilities also took on the responsibilities of paid employment. What had been viewed as a small problem for some families now became a problem for most families, and as such warranted attention from the society at large. Moreover, some countries have begun to recognize that this is really not just a problem for women, but that most adults—male and female—who have or expect to have children, are likely to have dual responsibilities at work and at home.

Now, as the United States begins to face the implications of this social revolution we, too, are experiencing, Americans might want to consider what is being done in other countries to respond to the needs of working mothers and working fathers—or working parents—with young children.

What follows is a selected picture of developments in Europe—what exists in several different countries in the way of both formal and informal responses to this new family life-style. Here, we are discussing countries in which the female labor force participation rates are slightly less than (as in the Federal Republic of Germany), about the same as (as in France), or higher than (as in Sweden) the U.S. rate.

The material is presented in this chapter to inform, to stimulate, and to challenge the reader. It is neither a full report of what is available nor a systematic presentation. For that, we refer you to more detailed reports and analyses of child-care policy and programs provided elsewhere.[1] Nor are we suggesting that Americans adopt lock, stock and barrel what exists elsewhere. What we are assuming, however, is that those of us who are experiencing this life-style directly, or experiencing it indirectly through our children, are curious about how others manage what clearly is a complicated and demanding way of life. Eventually, we too will have to develop our own solutions; but these programs from other countries may offer inspiration, raw material, or models.

Child Care Services

Needless to say, child care is the most important issue for working mothers in every country. As in the United States, it is more of a problem for women with preschool-age children. However, for most women, in most European countries, care of children from about age three to compulsory school entry (five, six, or seven, depending on the country) is far less of a problem than it is for American women. That is because most children of this age, in most of these countries, attend voluntarily a free, public preschool program, covering the normal school day; and they attend such programs regardless of whether or not their parents work. Although administered separately, most of these are part of the public education systems. In F.R. Germany, however, the programs may be operated by voluntary organizations and church groups, even though publicly subsidized, while in Sweden and Finland the programs are administered within a separate, freestanding preschool system.

It is not that children of this age are not attending similar programs in the United States. More than half (60 percent) are. However, except for the high percentage of five-year-olds in public kindergartens, most of these programs are private and unsubsidized, often last only a part-day (less than the standard school day), and still only serve less than half of the three- and four-year-olds. In contrast, the European picture for three- to five-year-olds goes something like this: More than 95 percent of children this age in France attend a public preschool program from about 8:30 in the morning to 4:00 in the afternoon. This program is free, except for lunch for those children whose parents wish them to have lunch at school, and for the special supplementary program (covering the hours from 7:00 A.M. until school opening, school closing to 6:00 P.M., and Wednesdays), which exists in many schools for the children of working parents. Parents are charged income-tested fees for this part of the program.

Similar preschool programs (with as extensive coverage) exist in Belgium, while in F.R. Germany about 75 percent of the three- to five-year-olds are in kindergartens. Like the standard school day in Germany, however, kindergarten may only cover 8:00 A.M. to 1:00 P.M., but a growing number of all schools, especially in working-class neighborhoods, cover a full day, specifically to assure care and activities for the children of working parents.

Although coverage (the numbers of children enrolled) is much lower in Sweden, a higher percentage of Swedish children are in programs that cover a full day, and, perhaps most important, all these preschool programs are public, heavily subsidized by the government, and thus free or at very low cost for parents.

It is not that there are not excellent nursery school programs and day care centers in the United States, but that there are many, many more such programs in these countries. For the most part, far more children can participate in such programs, if their parents wish them to; and the programs receive extensive public subsidies and thus are free or very inexpensive to parents. Furthermore, in all of these countries these programs are viewed as good for children—indeed, as essential for children and their optimum development—regardless of whether their parents are working, although there may be special programs supplementing the normal schoolday program, for the children of working parents, when the hours of school and work do not coincide.

To provide some sense of what these programs are like, we offer illustrations from France and Sweden. We have selected these two countries because France has an extraordinarily diverse array of child-care services, and the most comprehensive coverage of all Western countries, while Sweden has the most consistently high-quality programs, although its coverage is far less extensive.

The French *école maternelle* is a public preschool program that accepts children from the age of two to six. All four- and five-year-olds and more than 80 percent of the three-year-olds attend this program, and 32 percent of the two-year-olds, primarily those aged two and a half to three. The French VIIth National

Plan projected the expansion of this program to serve all three-year-olds and 45 percent of the two-year-olds by the early 1980s. In contrast, the Swedish preschool program is directed first at providing very high-quality care for the children of working parents and only subsequently expanding coverage for all children. However, Swedish female labor force participation is close to twice the French rate, although most French women work full time while most Swedish women work part time. Regardless, France offers the most extensive preschool coverage for three- to six-year-olds of any country in the world; and many French view this program as the "jewel" in their educational system.

In addition to the *école maternelle* the French have a very extensive day care program, administered under the auspices of the health ministry, for children, aged about three months to three years, of working mothers. This program is free for children of low-income families, and for others fees are income-related. Close to one-third of the children under three are in some form of out-of-home care, about half in day care centers or the *école maternelle* and half in licensed family day care homes. Indeed, France leads the world in the extensiveness of its licensed family day care arrangements.

The diversity among the French programs—as to program types and program quality—is truly astonishing. We saw programs that ranged from the best observed in any country to close to the worst. Despite this, child-care programs in France are needed and wanted, and clearly will continue to expand.

In contrast to the French administrative distinction in its child-care programs at age three, Swedish publicly subsidized child-care services are all provided through one separate, free-standing preschool program, serving children aged six months to seven years. Some of these programs also have a related supplementary school "leisure time" program for primary school children.

We offer a U.S. observers' view of these programs below.

VISITING THE *ÉCOLE MATERNELLE* IN FRANCE

In part because of the extensiveness of the *écoles maternelles* in France, it would be hard to describe a completely "typical" program, although after several visits one can begin to identify obvious similarities. They all tend to be relatively large, with what seems to an American to be very big groups or "classes" with surprisingly few teachers. A standard class has thirty-five children enrolled (although it may be higher) with one teacher and one "helper." Given the usual number of absentees, the average daily attendance is between twenty and twenty-five.

A PRESCHOOL IN PARIS

We visited one school in Paris that was located in a very poor neighborhood. Three hundred children, including a very high proportion of immigrant children, especially North Africans, attended the school. The director told us that she thought the number was too high for the facility and that she had been pressuring the Ministry, unsuccessfully thus far, to reduce the number. Through some personal manipulations of records, she expected to reduce the total enrollment the following year to 225, a number she viewed as more appropriate for the facility (which is in fact the standard size for most *écoles maternelles* in France). Her attitude was that given the size of the child population in this community another school should be opened regardless.

The building itself was more than a hundred years old and clearly had not been modernized since it was built, except for the bathrooms and kitchen facilities. It would not be an acceptable facility by most American fire standards. There was a steep wooden staircase leading from the first to the second floor, and there were wooden floors upstairs. The rooms on each floor were enormous, with extraordinarily high ceilings. Indeed, a four-story facility could easily have been constructed out of this one, if it were modernized.

The director was an extremely competent and dedicated woman who had administered the facility for several years and had worked in the *école maternelle* system for many years previously. She supervised the nine teachers at the school, in addition to kitchen and other custodial staff, and a psychologist who was assigned to the school part time.

The young preschoolers at this school were poor, immigrant, and racially mixed. More than half lived in homes without inside toilets. Many were from single-parent families. Many were from families we would describe as multiproblem, disorganized, and certainly deprived. The children attended school five and a half days a week, including Wednesday, when French schools are traditionally closed, and Saturday mornings, when French schools are traditionally open. And most attended the school from 8:30 A.M. to 6:00 P.M. The director was convinced that the experience for these children was an excellent one generally, facilitating their development and their adjustment to primary school subsequently.

There were thirty-five children in each class, with one staff person, and nine such classes on the two floors of the building. The rooms were large, and there seemed to be an enormous number of children to be coped with by only one teacher in each room. Yet despite this, many activities were going on: The children all seemed busy and happy and chattering, and the noise level was not unduly high. On the other hand, this was clearly an educational facility. The staff were trained teachers; the work shown to us by several teachers was fairly conventional in terms of the kinds of pictures the children drew and the types of stories they were encouraged to tell. Each child had a folder in which his/her work from the last several months was kept, so that it could be shown to his/her parents, too. It looked to us very much like a kindergarten class in a public school in an old area of one of our larger cities.

We visited one of the "middle" groups of three- and four-year-olds, who now, in late spring, were all four years old or a little older. Thirty-five children were registered for this class, but normally twenty to twenty-five attended. On the day we visited, there were twenty-one children. Chairs were arranged for all the children around three clusters of tables; however, only nine were seated, crayoning or stringing bead necklaces at the tables. The teacher's desk was in one corner of the room. The three other corners were clearly designed for specific types of small group play, and all were occupied. One corner was set up for a play kitchen, a second for a play house, and a third, with a table and a wardrobe. Four children were playing a game that involved two inside the wardrobe while the others played around the table. One child was resting on a mattress in the "play house" corner.

We asked the teacher how she managed all these children. She laughed and said, "Sometimes it's difficult. Now, when the weather is good, it's easier because the children can also run around and play outside, too."

There were two outside play areas. The one for the younger children, with a very large sandbox, was in the building quadrangle, which we crossed as we entered the school. We counted sixty pails and shovels and about three dozen rakes lying around in the sandbox before the children came out to play. It was clear that this would be enormously crowded when the younger group was present, and indeed, later on, we saw the children playing there. Although they were clearly having a good time, it was crowded.

A fairly typical schoolyard was available for the older preschool children. We saw about eighty four- and five-year-olds playing under the supervision of one teacher. It seemed terribly stark with no play equipment and a barren, grassless area. We were told that earlier there had been outside playthings, including swings and large rubber tires, but there were too many accidents, so they were removed. No effort had been made to do anything creative with the outside space. There was no chalk available for the children to play with, no painted shuffleboard courts, no hopscotch, no balls, no jumprope. In effect there was nothing for the children to do except run around and shout and fight. From our point of view there were simply too many children, in too small a space, with too little for them to do, and too few staff to supervise them.

IN ANOTHER TOWN

We visited a very different program located in one of France's most famous "new towns," on the edge of Grenoble in southeastern France, close to the border of Switzerland. This prototypical new town was built at the end of the 1960s on what formerly had been the city airport. Magnificent views of snow-capped Alps surround the community. The development contains a cluster of high-rise and medium-rise buildings, situated around a large park providing the central recreational facility for the whole community. Housing and commercial facilities (stores, banks, and shopping areas), as well as school, health, recreational, and community facilities are all integrated within each of two of the three completed "quarters."

The first group among the 18,000 residents moved in in 1972; when the third quarter is completed the population will total 28,000—9,000 in each quarter. Each of the high-rise residential buildings includes both rented as well as individually owned apartments, in the proportion of approximately two to one. All the residential and community facilities are publicly subsidized. The central parklike area is completely closed off to vehicular traffic. Only pedestrians can use the walks and space, which also are totally accessible to all the schools, preschools, and day care centers. Thus children of all ages play in the open areas, which the local residents use for strolling, sitting, or walking to work.

Each quarter has a total population of about 9,000, including 2,000 children. The residents are largely middle and working class, with a large group of North African immigrants.

In the quarter we visited, there were one secondary school, five elementary schools serving about 200 children each, five *écoles maternelles* serving a little under 200 children each, one *crèche collective* (a day care center for children aged three and under serving 60 children), one *crèche familial* (an agency-supervised group, family day care home for the same age group) serving 80 children, and one *halte-garderie* (a part-time child-care center) serving a maximum of 20 children at any one time, but about 200 overall.

Almost all the children aged two to six attend the *école maternelle* in this community—more specifically, all three- four- and five-year-olds and 90 percent of the two-year-olds. The size of the school as well as the group size are much smaller than those programs we visited in Paris. Staff-to-child ratios are higher, and the administrators of the local elementary and preschool systems have made creative use of existing funds by amalgamating two different programs in order to "upgrade" the *école maternelle*. More specifically, the community had, in addition to the five *écoles maternelles*, one other public preschool program just for two- to four-year-olds, which was designed to be smaller and have more staff, since it served younger children. By integrating this program into the larger preschool programs, they were able to improve significantly the quality of the larger program.

The *école maternelle* was located in a very attractive modern facility which resembled a cluster of beehives, all on one story. The program was open twelve hours a day, five and a half days a week, from 7:00 A.M. to 7:00 P.M. Monday through Friday. Children may have meals there and there is full coverage for non-school hours, including the summer months. The 9-to-5 part of the program is free to parents except for the actual meals, because this core part of the program is the public preschool, available free to all children. Parents pay for the two-hour units from 7:00 to 9:00 A.M., from 5:00 to 7:00 P.M., and for the meals. The fees are income-related and range for the two-hour units from one-half franc to three francs for each day. The maximum fee for the meals is seven francs per day.[2]

The main "teaching" staff are present from 9:00 A.M. until noon and from 2:00 to 5:00 P.M., although several stay through lunch. Additional trained child-care staff work in two shifts, from 7:00 A.M. until 2:30 P.M. and from 11:00 A.M. to 7:00 P.M., thus ensuring an overlap at meal times, for purposes of staff communication as well as for adequate staffing at the most difficult time of the day. Since this community has a very high percentage of families with two wage-earners and single-parent families where the sole parent works, there is very extensive use of the supplementary school program. The overall staffing pattern results in one professional staff member for every seventeen registered children, in contrast to the usual 1:35, plus assistants.

The preschool we visited served 120 children in 35 groups of 40 each (instead of 75, which is standard in France), divided as follows: one group of twelve two- and three-year-olds, with one teacher and an assistant; a second group of fourteen three- and four-year-olds, with one teacher and an assistant; and a third group of fourteen four- and five-year-olds, staffed by two teachers. Each group was housed in one of these "beehive" arrangements, which permitted the group to be subdivided into two, in separate rooms. The physical structure was extraordinarily attractive, with plenty of room for active play, quiet play, water play, games of hide-and-seek, and corners to rest in. Many different types of activities were going on at the same time, and the children clearly were receiving a great deal of individual attention from staff. We watched one young assistant sitting on the floor and holding a group of four three-year-olds fully entranced as she read them a story. There were also several small tables and chairs in the room and an extensive assortment of beautifully designed and crafted toys in bright colors. A couple of parents came in, one to bring a child, another to visit, and it was clear that this kind of accessibility to parents was all part of a pervasive philosophy encouraging active parent participation and involvement. Here, we saw healthy and happy children in as stimulating and nurturing an environment as we saw anywhere.

We were particularly struck, in France, by the fact that neither the socioeconomic characteristics of the neighborhood in which a program was located nor the "wealth" of the families served seemed to correlate with what we viewed as the "quality" level of the child-care programs. We saw physically beautiful programs in affluent neighborhoods serving largely professional and upper-middle-class families, which seemed to us to be rigid, authoritarian, inadequately equipped, and insensitive to the needs and wants of children. Some such programs seemed to lack what we would view as the minimum elements of an adequate child-care program: interaction between staff and children; concern for a child's feelings, safety, well-being. We saw programs in poor neighborhoods, located in old, decrepit buildings, serving immigrant children primarily, which were warm, exciting, caring environments with excellent and appropriate equipment, where staff spent extensive time and individualized attention with each child despite what seemed to us to be large groups. And we saw the reverse, too. If we were to assess what we learned, we would probably conclude that the single most important fact in determining the quality of a child-care program in France is the ability, philosophy, and personality of the overall director. In general, France has stressed coverage and quantitative adequacy of provision, primarily; and clearly the extensiveness of the children served is a tribute to this. And by and large the children seemed happy and healthy. France, now, is increasingly turning toward improving the quality of the child-care program. We saw this in the growing debate regarding reduction in the size of the *maternelle* classes; in the encouragement of innovative and experimental neighborhood child-care programs which include preschool, day care centers, and maternal and child health programs; in the changing nature of the *crèche collective*—the day care centers for children under three—as they become more open, spontaneous environments, and less "health"-oriented. Finally, we saw this in the recent expansion of licensing requirements for family day care. Now, anyone who takes care of a child outside of the child's own home, even a relative, must be licensed. All of this is part of the current French policy to upgrade the quality of care that all children, but especially the children of working mothers, receive outside of their own homes.

We conclude this picture of the diversity of child-care services in France with a description of a *crèche collective* (a day care center), a *mini-creche* (a very small day care center, more like what we in America would call a family day care group home), and family day care generally.

Visiting *Crèches* in France

As we indicated earlier, day care centers (or *crèches*, to use the French term) serve children under three while the preschool programs serve children two to six. Thus there is an overlap in France for children aged two and three. Increasingly, to the extent that space is available, children this age attend the *maternelle*. These preschool programs, which are under the administrative authority of the Ministry of Education, are free and serve all children regardless of whether or not their mothers work. The day care centers are under the Ministry of Health and are free to children from low-income families but charge income-related fees (though less than most because of heavy subsidies) to all others, and serve the children of working mothers. Since just about any child aged three or older whose parents wish it, can, and indeed does, attend a preschool program, French policy now is to support the expansion of care for those under three—more places in the *maternelles* for two- and three-year-olds and expanded provisions in *crèches* and with *nourrices* (family day care mothers).

The standard center has places for sixty children in four groups of fifteen children each. Average daily attendance is between forty-five and fifty. The staff-to-child ratio is one professional staff member to five infants (children who are not yet walking), or eight toddlers (children under three who are walking). Staff usually include an administrative director, eight to ten "nurses," a cook, and one or two custodial workers. *Crèches* are open twelve hours per day from 7:00 A.M. to 7:00 P.M. Most centers have long waiting lists for admission.

Almost all *crèches* in France are neighborhood-based; there are only a few which are located at the work place. Day care at the work place is a declining phenomenon throughout all Europe, as it becomes increasingly clear that parents prefer childcare arrangements near their homes, not at the work place. The problems with work place arrangements, according to parents who have been interviewed, include the following: a general dislike of being tied to a particular job in order to assure care for a child; exposing a young child to long travel at peak "commuting" hours; getting a child to the center when a parent is ill; restricting a child's friendships to the children of other workers and isolating a child from neighborhood friendships. Thus, all new centers are neighborhood-based, in or adjacent to residential areas.

Center "groups" are generally age-related, with one group of infants under one year; a second group of "beginning walkers" aged about one year to eighteen months; a third aged eighteen months to two years; and a fourth aged two to three.

The *crèche* and the agency-administered family day care homes are especially attractive to parents, because the programs are most supervised and thus more likely to be of higher quality. However, they are also liked by parents because public subsidies assure that the cost to parents is reasonable. In contrast, privately arranged-for care is quite expensive.

A CRÈCHE IN PARIS

We visited a *crèche* in Paris, housed, like the *maternelle*, in a nineteenth-century building which had been only somewhat modernized when it was turned into a *crèche* twenty years ago. The current directress had been there for two years. The previous one had administered the program for twelve years, until her retirement, and had been particularly instrumental in changing the *creche* from a very rigid and traditional health-oriented program to its present more relaxed and "developmental" focus. All the other staff had been at the center for several years and, we were told, staff turnover generally was quite low.

This *crèche*, with places for forty-five children, was somewhat smaller than the standard "maximum" size of sixty. There were three groups: an infants' group with eighteen children aged two months to one year and three trained staff; a middle group of fourteen children aged sixteen months to two years, also with three staff; and an older group of thirteen children aged two to three with one staff person and a trainee. These older children were all close to their third birthday and within the next few months would be entering the *école maternelle*, which was adjacent to the *crèche*.

The *crèche* is open twelve hours a day (even though most of the children attend for about eight or nine hours) and staff work an eight-hour day. The staffing pattern tends to be: one person at the beginning of the day, one at the end, two between 9:00 A.M. and 5:00 P.M. , and a full complement of three in the middle of the day, between 11:00 A.M. and 3:00 P.M.

This *crèche* was structured in the form of a long rectangle with a central hallway and a series of rooms off it on either side. There was a small enclosed outside area for play. The first room to the left as one entered the hallway was the kitchen. Here the bottles were prepared for the infants who were fed on "demand" or following whatever schedule parents indicated their child was used to. All meals were prepared there, since the director does not like to use "prepared" food and prefers fresh fruits and vegetables for the children. When we looked into the kitchen we saw a staff member preparing "play dough" (2 parts wheat, 1 part salt, 1 part vegetable oil), thus providing a play material that would not harm any child who might decide to taste it.

The next room was the babies' room. The youngest here was two months old, but most were about one year (since this was close to the "end" of the year). Cribs were lined up around two walls, on very high legs, which in turn were padded, so the children could crawl around freely under them, as well as in the open area in the center of the room. The floor was made of a soft (and warm) composition material. There were no playpens or other arrangements to confine the children, so apart from two infants (two and six months old) who were asleep in the cribs, all the other children were walking, crawling, or sitting on the floor, playing with toys or with each other. Occasionally, one or two "older" children would come visit for a while from another room, and they were encouraged to play with the babies, too. It was clear that although there was a great deal of activity the atmosphere was relaxed and the children were constantly supervised by the three staff members. Each of these was "responsible" for a particular group of six and spent time talking to and playing with each child individually.

When it was lunchtime, the cook, the sewing lady, and a woman who helped clean the *crèche* all pitched in so that no child had to wait while others were fed. Even in this infants' group, several of the children who were about a year old were already able to feed themselves.

We visited next the middle group of fourteen children aged sixteen months to two years. The children were at two tables, the four at one table busily fingerpainting and six at the other working on the playdough that we had earlier seen made in the kitchen. There were four mattresses off in one corner of the room, available in case a child felt like resting. One child was lying down when we came in and then later joined the fingerpainting group. In another corner was a table with a cloth over it, where a few children were playing house.

The children were encouraged to be very independent, and several were able to toilet themselves. While we were present, one little boy walked off to one of the small-size toilets in a bathroom area off the playroom, took care of himself, and then returned. Afterwards, we discussed the question of toilet training with the staff members present. They said that in contrast to the approach used five or ten years ago, there is a very relaxed and permissive attitude now. No effort is made at "formal" toilet training. However, at somewhere around eighteen to twenty months, if a child evinces any interest, staff members put the child on the potty before and after meals. In general, children seemed to train themselves. Since they see older children using the potty or the toilet, they have peer role models to emulate as soon as they are able to exercise control themselves.

Mealtimes are always of particular interest when visiting a child-care facility. As one might expect, they were of special interest in France. A small sign near the *crèche* entrance indicated what the menu was for that day and the next, so parents could note what their children ate. For us it was an unusual experience, because for the first time we saw institutional food in a child-care facility that was beautifully arranged and served, and, as we discovered later, delicious! Clearly, eating was important not just in terms of nutrition but as a socializing experience. All these children fed themselves. Five were at each of two tables, while the four slightly younger ones were at a third. The meal included hardboiled eggs, mashed carrots, puréed green vegetables, peeled apple quarters, and banana slices. Although the children managed spooning from plate to mouth with a certain amount of mess on the side, by and large they showed remarkable dexterity.

The older group comprised thirteen children close to age three, all of whom would enter the *maternelle* in three months, after the summer. One full-time staff member was present in addition to a student trainee. Within the last few months the children had been taken several times to visit the *maternelle* they would attend in the fall and had met their "teacher" there.

In this room were four clusters of small tables, with two children at one table busily engaged in water play. Two others were seated at another table, listening to a story. Three more were playing house in a corner of the room where something like a small picket fence marked off an area where there was a miniature kitchen, a stove, a sink, and a table. Two others were climbing on a series of stacked wooden boxes.

Wherever we looked in the center, we saw lots of equipment, used imaginatively and creatively, to encourage children to play, to stimulate them, and to provide them with the freedom to move in various directions on their own while in a protected environment. Staff talked to the children and were obviously available to them and concerned about them; but the children were also clearly learning from one another in their play activities.

Once again mealtime was a fascinating experience to observe. The children at each table were served by the staff with a platter from which each child served himself or herself. Some children took several spoonfuls, while others took smaller portions. One little boy took two halves of hardboiled egg while the others took only one. It was clear that the children were encouraged to feel that they could control the size of the portions they were getting and were helped to be self-sufficient in handling their eating. Yet none took an inadequate portion of anything. We were told that the menu is always sufficiently varied so that if a child does not like one particular item, an alternative is available. And almost all the plates were completely empty by the end of the meal. The children in this group were also provided with a small bottle of water as well as with a glass, so that they could begin to learn how to handle "pouring." Some of the children did pour the water into the glass while others drank from the bottle directly, and one asked to have his water poured for him.

We were especially interested to learn that two staff members had their own children in the *crèche* and that several others had had their children in attendance in previous years. Several children had older siblings who attended previously, too.

Parents are encouraged to visit the *crèche* if they let the staff know in advance. We talked to one mother who was present for a while when we first arrived. Her enthusiasm for the program

and for the experience it provided her year-old son was bound-
less. After our visit, we understood her attitude completely. We
felt the same way.

MINI-CRÈCHES AND FAMILY DAY CARE IN FRANCE

Because of the growing demand for more places in *crèches*,
and the capital costs involved in establishing new ones as well as
the time it takes to do so, there are several innovations in child
care now supported in France. One such development is a *mini-
crèche* program, developed in response to the problems of time
and cost, but also in order to provide a child-care facility in a
neighborhood that could not support a larger *crèche* and thus
would otherwise have no group facility available. These *mini-
crèches* may be located in an apartment or even a small house in
a suburban community. They each serve twelve children, usually
under age two, with two staff members.

These programs are described as a cross between family day
care and center care. Here too, the style and quality of the program reflect the leadership of the senior staff person more than
anything else. Visiting several of these in one medium-size city in
France underscored the range that is possible in any type of facility. Clearly, size and scale, by themselves, do not determine
what a program is like. The *mini-crèche* can be antiseptic, rigid,
and authoritarian, or relaxed and spontaneous; staff may talk to
and play with children, or not; parents may be encouraged to
visit, ask questions, and be kept informed about their child's development, or not.

Similarly, we talked to administrators of the agency-operated
family day care program and to some parents who used privately
arranged family day care. Although the current policy in France
is to give equal satus to both family day care and center care, the
reality is that family day care is still more extensive, and there is a
heated debate as to which type of care is better for children
and/or preferred by parents. All family day care must be licensed
now, and this regulation is increasingly enforced. Moreover, the
family day care mothers are limited to caring for a maximum of

three children; although the national average is lower—two children.

The arguments that some parents express in favor of family day care are: There may be more flexibility about hours; there is greater likelihood that a slightly ill child can be cared for in such an arrangement (rather than a parent's being required to care for the child at home); there may be a more "family"-like atmosphere; and where immigrant and working-class families are concerned, the family day care mother is more likely to come from the same class and culture as the child's own family.

The arguments against family day care and for center care are: It is easier to monitor the quality of center care (it is almost impossible to supervise what goes on daily in a family day care home); the staff is better trained; the children have a wider choice of staff to relate to in the event that there is someone they do not like; and most important, children have the opportunity of having a group experience with other children, something which many believe to be extremely beneficial even for very young children.

Needless to say, this debate occurs in France and most of Europe only for children under age two or two and a half. No one argues in favor of family day care for children older than this. Indeed, children from two and a half or three to six are considered to be deprived if they do not have a group preschool experience. Moreover, the cost issue is becoming progressively less important in deciding between center and family day care, since operating costs are largely a matter of staff costs, which may be even higher for family day care than for center care. (If staff are adequately paid, have vacations and other fringe benefits, and take depreciation for their homes and equipment, family day care has higher labor costs. Since labor represents over 70 percent of day care center costs, the high staff: child ratios of family day care could make it a very expensive program to operate.) The ultimate question may be who bears the burden of costs, government or the individual family? In this context, *private* family day care is of course "cheaper" for the government, because it bears no share of the costs; but publicly subsidized family day care, which is extensive in France, already is almost as costly as center care. There

may be other reasons for continued support of family day care as
a special program for some children, but this we will return to
later.

Preschool in Sweden

For a different picture of child-care services, we turn to the Swedish preschool programs. In contrast to the French, the Swedish
program makes no administrative distinctions regarding programs for this age group. There is one integrated program for all
children aged six months to seven years, administered by a separate child-care agency, not part of either the health or the educational system. Moreover, the Swedish policy explicitly favors
center or group programs for all children regardless of age.
However, the extensiveness of places for children is far, far less
than in France. Indeed, although it is something of an oversim-
plification, Sweden has clearly stressed quality of preschool at
the expense of quantity. Sweden has perhaps the highest-quality
publicly subsidized child-care program in the world. Yet given its
very high rate of female labor force participation, coverage is
low, with perhaps only about half the children aged three to sev-
en in some form of out-of-home care and about 30 percent of the
under-threes in care (half in publicly subsidized care and half in
private, informal arrangements). Government officials state that
over the next few years the number of places will expand to cover
all the children of working mothers—the Swedish priority group.
However, given the fact that almost two-thirds of the women are
in the labor force (although only half work full time) it seems
highly unlikely that coverage will be adequate in the near future.

A PRESCHOOL IN STOCKHOLM

We visited one child-care center[3] which was located in the "service center" or shopping center area of a large housing development in suburban Stockholm. The center serves children of resi-

dents primarily, in a specially constructed facility. The very attractive, low, one story building is very typical of such specially designed Swedish child-care facilities surrounded by extensive grounds, with separate gardens and play areas for the younger and older children, including a sandbox and outdoor equipment appropriate for each age group. The facility and the setting highlighted a pervasive characteristic of the Swedish programs. In every program we visited, in contrast to the French programs, the facilities were very modern and there was great emphasis on outdoor space and play areas. Clearly, Sweden has a much more recent history of formal child care than France.

Sixty children are the maximum permitted in this type of facility, but the number varies depending on the facility size. None are larger, although many are smaller. This center had fifty-four children enrolled in four groups, as follows: one group of fifteen five- to seven-year-olds, a second group of fifteen three- to five-year-olds, a third group of twelve children from one and a half to three, and a fourth group of twelve aged six to eighteen months. The staff total eighteen; however, several of these work only part time, so the actual total, in full-time equivalents, is twelve and a half. The staff are divided equally among the groups, except that the group aged eighteen months to three years has one more adult and the oldest group one less. The two-year-olds are viewed as particularly demanding and therefore needing more staff. There is one young man on staff, too. Sweden is the only country in Europe where we saw male child-care workers, and there is a very conscious effort to recruit young men as staff. The Swedes are convinced that it is essential for young children to have male "teachers" if they are to develop nonstereotypical views of male and female roles.

The director is hoping next year to restructure the program into four equal "sibling" groups, an increasingly popular program concept in Swedish child-care programs. This means each group would include thirteen or fourteen children ranging in age from six months to seven years, instead of the conventional age-related groups that exist in most countries.[4] The idea is that this is a much more natural environment for children and that it is helpful for a child's development to be exposed to children of dif-

ferent ages. As part of this approach, some centers also have programs for school-age children, after school, when these older
children are encouraged to help with the care of the younger ones
and to play with them.

The facility itself was located on a hill and constructed as a
kind of split-level house, with the ground floor used for the three-
to seven-year-olds, who had their outdoor play area on that level,
and the second floor for the younger children whose play area
was adjacent, at the top of the hill. Each floor had three rooms,
plus a bathroom area and a kitchen. One room was a central area
where the children entered, where all could play together. Here
were large wooden boxes for climbing and plenty of toys and
games. Two smaller rooms opened off the central room. Where
the younger children were concerned, they were used for resting.
Since the weather was sunny and mild when we visited, all the
children were outside, some wading in a large inflated rubber
pool, several of the older ones playing in a tree house, others in
the sandbox, and three sitting on a blanket listening to a story.

The staff, who all have either pediatric nursing training, or,
for the older children and increasingly for all, special training in
early childhood education, were young, enthusiastic, and dedicated. The center has been in existence for eleven years. The director has been there since the beginning, and most of the staff
have worked there for several years. We were told that staff turnover is quite low. As in France, the staff work an eight-hour day
and a forty-hour week. These programs, too, are open for twelve
hours a day, here from 6:00 A.M. to 6:00 P.M., although most children spend eight to ten hours a day at the center. The staffing
pattern is staggered and changes over the year so that all staff
work each schedule. The usual pattern is for one person to be
there when the center opens, a second to arrive a half-hour or an
hour later, depending on when children arrive, and a full complement of staff to be at the center from 9:00 A.M. to 2:00 P.M. At
that time staff begin to leave. However, there are usually several
who remain until closing time, and even after, because the staff
clean up, meet to make special plans for the next day, or to discuss problems or concerns with regard to a particular child. Staff
meetings are frequent. Meetings with parents are held regularly,

but much less frequently, at most once a month. Staff report that working parents complain that they have no time to come to meetings.

A PRESCHOOL IN THE COUNTRYSIDE

We visited another preschool program on the outskirts of a beautiful old seaport on the southern coast of Sweden, about 350 miles south of Stockholm. Although almost every child-care center we visited in Sweden was beautifully designed and often situated in an unusually attractive setting, this was among the loveliest. Located in a middle-class residential community of detached one-family houses, the center itself looked like an unusually large and sprawling private home with a well kept garden. There were beautiful trees, a well tended flowering rock garden, and several large sandboxes placed unobtrusively in a natural setting of grass and pebbles. Because it was a very warm day early in June, there were also several large plastic tubs filled with water located around the grounds, and the children were playing in the tubs and running around in the grass. The center appeared even more like a private home with a children's party going on, because there seemed to be a very large number of adults for a relatively small number of children. The director, an attractive thirty-year-old woman, had organized the center four years ago at the suggestion of the municipality, beginning with thirty children— twenty who participated in the full-day program and ten in the part-day program. This is a rather conservative semirural community. Previously, there had been a small part-day preschool program for five- and six-year-old children, and only private family day care for the children of working parents. With a large increase in the number of working mothers in the area, the municipality decided to establish a preschool center-based program. The director approached the parents involved in the existing program, who initially were not sure they wanted their children in the same program as the other children but agreed to try it. Today there is great enthusiasm on the part of all the parents, many of whom are now quite active in the program. Recently the program has expanded to include ten children between seven months and three years, in addition to the thirty three- to seven-year-olds now participating, and five more will be admitted in the fall. In addition, two more centers like this have opened elsewhere in the area. This one, however, is the only one that operates as a "sibling" group for the three- to seven-year-olds as well as for those aged seven months to three years. There are now forty children in the program in three groups of fifteen, fifteen, and ten with eight full-time staff, two part-time, and additional trainees. (Full enrollment is forty-eight children—eighteen, eighteen, and twelve; average attendance is never over forty.)

The center is open twelve months a year, twelve hours a day, five days a week. Only one child is there for the whole twelve hours; most attend for eight to ten hours. Children come from the neighborhood, but not necessarily within walking distance. Staff work a forty-hour week and an eight-hour day, rotating early and late schedules, and working staggered hours similar to those in the Stockholm program described above. Here, too, between 9:30 A.M. and 2:30 P.M. there is a full complement of staff, with fewer during the earlier and later hours. All staff share in all tasks. As a consequence, the director and child-care professionals take turns at cooking, cleaning, and so forth, and the cooks and cleaning women participate in child care, too.

A typical day for the three- to seven-year-olds involves the center's opening at 6:00 A.M.. Between 6:00 A.M. and 7:30 A.M. children straggle in at irregular intervals, gathering with the one staff member present in one room, playing at whatever appeals to them. At 7:30 A.M. the second staff member arrives, and if the group is large enough it is divided in two—otherwise all remain together. At 8:00 A.M. the staff give the children breakfast. At 9:00 A.M. all gather together in the big central activity room, which is set up with all sorts of heavy-duty climbing equipment and really provides a substitute for outdoor activities during the larger part of the year when it is too cold and too dark to go outside to play early in the morning. This is the only time in the day that all the children are together. New children are introduced then. New equipment and toys are demonstrated, and the children can try them out. The five- and six-year-olds are usually separated after this for more formal "learning" activities.[5] Children who are identified as having particular problems of one sort or another may be singled out then also for special attention. Although it is described as a sibling group, the three- to five-year-olds and the five- to seven-year-olds tend to play together. Sometimes special excursions are carried out in the morning, depending on the weather and the time of year, to visit the seaside, the port, the mountains, forests, nearby factories, shipyards, and so forth.

At 11:00 A.M. the children have lunch in separate groups and the staff have lunch with the children, after which the children who wish to, rest. The afternoon begins with a quiet play time, when staff read to the children who are not resting. Later, if the weather is good, the children go outside again to play. By 4:00 P.M. the departures begin, and by 6:00 P.M. all have left, only the staff remaining to clean up for the next day.

Approximately ten new children enter each year when the ten oldest children begin school in mid-August. Parents of the new children are requested to bring their children to visit during the summer, and they may participate in some of the special group excursions, too. Parents are encouraged to take off one to two and a half days from work to help children make the transition to the program, and they are entitled to time off from work, with pay, in order to do this. New children are given special attention by the staff. The usual approach is to begin the new children two at a time, so that no child feels unique in his "new status," yet the staff can give ample extra attention to the new ones.

As the director explained to us, the goals of the program are "to complement home and family life by providing good care and a safe and secure environment in which children will develop, be happy, and become independent, self-reliant, problem-solving individuals." Here, too, several staff members had or have had their own children in the program.

The children were beautiful, sturdy youngsters. Not only were they obviously happy, but there was an astonishingly high degree of individuality among them, in manner, speech, play, and the way they related to one another and to the staff. We saw children who helped one another, several who together were building a "house" with wooden boards and blocks, a six-year-old who comforted a three-year-old when he fell down. Where the very young children were concerned, the major stress was on "enhancing the child's development within the normal daily routines of eating, dressing, bathing." Staff talk to children, even as they change a diaper or feed them. And often older children talk to them, too. As part of the program philosophy, much of normal household routine is maintained, and children and staff are incorporated into these activities. If the telephone rings a child may accompany the staff member who answers it. When a baby's bottle is prepared, a three-year-old may go along to observe and help. Children help clean the tables off after meals, explore how the vacuum cleaner works, and are generally encouraged to ask questions—and to receive answers. Although the youngest ones tend to be kept separate, at some time during the day they are visited by older children, who are encouraged to play with the little ones.

Although we visited several smaller programs, too, which enrolled only twenty-four or thirty children, we found none to be any more successful in individualizing the care and attention each child received that this one.

Although family day care is far more extensively used in Sweden than in France, it seems to be supported in part out of expediency and in part as a potentially therapeutic and "special" program for children with special needs. The Swedes do subsidize family day care by paying providers through the municipality and having parents pay fees to the appropriate agency. Some family day care homes are attached to centers, and children may spend a portion of the day in each. Family day care mothers may be trained and supervised by center staff, too. Certainly until there are adequate places in centers for all children whose parents want such care for them, some family day care will have to exist. Many prominent Swedes, however, are convinced that group care is preferable for most children. Fees are the same for both types of care, and the long-term prospectus is that family day care is certainly not a less expensive form of care than center-based child care. According to the Swedes, the operating costs of family day care are even higher than for center care, because the staff:child ratios are higher in the former. Once family day care mothers are trained, they want the same pay and fringe benefits as center staff. Since staff salaries are the largest item in child-care program costs (about 70 percent) any program with a high staff:child ratio is expensive. With family day care mothers limited to caring for a maximum of four children, these programs become quite expensive. Thus, ultimately the Swedes think family day care would be specifically for children who need a very small group experience, or handicapped children who require special care, but not for the average child, who needs and can benefit from a group experience.

An Unyielding Environment, an Unresponsive Society

If child care is the primary problem and concern of working mothers in the United States, the second important problem involves the pressure from an unyielding work environment in the face of child and family responsibilities. American women complain about the absence of any kind of support which would make it easier to manage work and home responsibilities simultaneously. Just as there is more extensive provision of publicly subsidized out-of-home child-care services in much of Europe, there is also more extensive provision of those benefits which may alleviate the most acute work-related stress. Once again, it is not that none of these benefits exist in the United States. Some do, but even when they do they exist only as part of the private fringe benefit systems in some industries, and therefore only concern a very small proportion of working women. In contrast, these benefits are provided by law in much of Europe and, therefore, cover all women.

To begin with, every country in Europe guarantees employed women the right to a leave from their jobs following childbirth. In addition, all provide a cash benefit, usually through the social security system, predicated on the assumption that maternity is a "normal" risk for a working woman requiring "protection"

against loss of earnings, just as protection is provided for against
unemployment or disability. In all these countries, women are
entitled to a minimum leave of three months, usually with six
weeks permitted to be taken before expected childbirth and eight
weeks after. The cash benefit is usually equal to—or close to—
full wages (up to whatever the maximum covered wage is under
social security) with a guarantee of job protection and seniority
during that time. Almost all countries also provide women with
the right to take an additional unpaid leave for about one year
or longer, with their jobs protected even though they receive no
monetary compensation.

Several countries have much more extensive versions of these
benefits, however. The Federal Republic of Germany now provides what is becoming increasingly the norm in Europe, a seven-
and-one-half-month paid maternity leave for employed women,
including six months after childbirth.

Sweden and, to a much less extent, Norway provide something of even greater interest to working parents: a special parent
insurance benefit under the social security system. This benefit,
like the paid maternity leave, is available only to parents at
childbirth or when a baby is adopted, to permit parents to remain at home and care for their new baby without suffering financial hardship as a consequence of lost wages. The Swedish
parent insurance covers nine months (up to six weeks for the
mother before expected childbirth), with close to full wage replacement and job protection for either parent. Moreover, this
cash benefit can be prorated and used to cover part-time work.

We met a young couple in Sweden with a two-year-old girl
who was now attending a preschool program. They explained to
us how they managed to care for their daughter themselves until
she was one year old. Eva, the mother, took off one month after
the baby was born. With flexitime to begin work early—or to
end late—and adjusting their lunch schedules, they continued to
share child care between them until the baby was one year old.
For the next year Eva managed to get permission to continue
working a six-hour day and arranged for a family day care
mother to care for the baby. Now the baby has begun to attend
a full-day program at the local preschool. Recent legislation,

which went into effect in 1979, has guaranteed the right to part-time work and a six-hour day to all parents of young children.

Several young Swedish couples told us how helpful they have found this parent insurance benefit. Indeed, another important part of it, which exists in several other countries also, is the provision for a specific number of days which an employee can take off, with close to full pay, if his or her young child is home ill and needs to be cared for. Here, too, in most countries only women are eligible for this benefit, but in Sweden either parent is eligible.

We have, of course, mentioned flexitime as a possible aid for working parents. Some companies in the United States are experimenting with flexitime, as is the federal government. F.R. Germany has introduced flexible work scheduling very extensively. With flexitime, workers have a wider choice of beginning and ending work hours. The usual arrangement is that if the standard work day begins at 9:00 A.M., employees can begin anytime between 7:00 A.M. and 11:00 A.M.; and if the usual closing time is 5:00 P.M., employees can elect to leave anytime between 3:00 P.M. and 7:00 P.M., as long as they put in an eight-hour day. This makes it possible, for example, for one parent to be at home until the children leave for school in the morning, while the other can reach home about the same time as they return from school in the afternoon. Some companies also permit further adjustments such as working an occasional ten-hour day in order to work less another day.

Another related effort at making it easier to manage home and work responsibilities is the new Swedish legislation mentioned above, which guarantees the right of part-time work with proportionate fringe benefits to parents with young children.

Although not directly related to coping more easily with work and family responsibilities, several other benefits exist throughout Europe that do take some of the stress out of parenting and family responsibilities generally. Among the most important of these benefits are:

• a free, public, high-quality maternal and child health service through which every woman receives hospitalization and medical care at childbirth, and every infant and young child re-

ceives regular checkups. Some countries, like England and
France, have "health visitors" who visit young mothers and children in their own homes. In addition, like other countries in Europe, they also have excellent neighborhood pediatric clinics
where children receive regular and frequent checkups. All these
countries have physicians attached to the child-care programs as
well.

- a child or family allowance, a cash benefit given to every
family based on the presence of children in the family. This benefit is provided in every industrialized country but the United
States and is often a great help to working parents by offering a
small supplement to what may otherwise be low wages.

Other Problems—but Where Are the Solutions?

The third and fourth most important problems mentioned by the
American mothers we interviewed were:

- the shortage of time in which to get the variety of family
  and home-related tasks accomplished
- the lack of help at home to fulfill these tasks

Here we see only a beginning of any attention to these problems both in the United States and in other countries. Indeed, it
is in relation to problems such as these that it becomes even
clearer that what we are seeing can no longer be addressed as a
"women's" problem but a problem for all men as well as women,
as all adults regardless of gender are increasingly likely to be in
the labor force and to be fulfilling family and parenting roles and
responsibilities too. The problem of the allocation of time as a
scarce resource and of the impact of household and family-related tasks which have to be accomplished within a limited
amount of time clearly requires a reassessment of intrafamily
roles. Here, the ultimate goal would be to facilitate greater equity between men and women within the family. Clearly, this can
occur only within the confines of individual interpersonal and in-
trafamilial relationships. However, existing public policies can

facilitate or impede some trend toward equity for women by the extent to which the work–family tension is defined as a problem for all adults, not only for women.

Historically, the division of labor within the family has been predicated on the assumption that women carry primary responsibility for child care and household tasks and responsibilities. Existing patterns of work for men reinforced this by making it difficult if not impossible for men to manage much in the way of home and family tasks, as home and work became more and more separate. The advent of women into paid employment outside the home did not change this role allocation. Instead, as we have indicated, the assumption was that women had "two jobs" to maintain while men had only one—the economic support of the family—even though increasingly this task was being shared or, in a growing number of families with only one parent, carried alone. The separation of work and home created a series of problems for men as workers, and for women and children and families in general, as the worlds of home and work became segregated and distinct domains. As women entered the labor force, it was assumed that they could cope with these separate domains by personal sacrifice; that is, women would overburden themselves by putting in longer work days and work weeks (carrying two jobs, even if only one was paid, required this); and they would achieve less status and lower compensation in the labor market, because they were constrained by time (and other things) and thus could not compete equally with men for the higher-paid and higher-status jobs. With more than half of all adult non-aged women in the labor force today in all industrialized countries, the picture is changing, especially as young women enter the labor market at the same time as young men, expecting to remain there, regardless of whether or not they have children. Equal opportunity in the labor market requires equity at home, especially in those roles which span home and employment. Failure to assess such equity has negative consequences for women, for children, for families—and, inevitably, as some men are discovering—for men, too. Ultimately, such failure will have negative consequences for the society at large also. Assuring equity requires attention to the interface of work and family life.

As we have indicated in our report, thus far in the United States what has occurred has been family members—adults and children—adapting to the reality of both parents in the labor force. In contrast, the European countries we have described, as well as many others, have begun to acknowledge the need for societal adaptation to this new family life-style; although most have focused on the issue as a problem for women only, a few have recognized that the concern is a larger one, for men as well as women—indeed for the whole society. And as more married women with young children enter the labor force, this trend must increase, as it becomes obvious that the labor force is made up of many working parents—not just individual men and women—who carry these dual responsibilities.

Clearly, the responsibility for the development of support systems for families, making it possible for adults to carry both sets of responsibilities at the same time, can only come from the society at large, with society using government as its instrument. Only through publicly guaranteed entitlements can all families benefit, not just some employees whose employers will then feel penalized as they make some special adjustments. Many Americans continue to believe that (a) the problem of managing work and family life is a problem for individuals to handle through informal or market place arrangements; (b) it is a women's problem; and (c) all governmental provisions with regard to policies should be limited to situations of pathology, deviance, or inadequacy. Only in relatively recent history have Americans acknowledged that old age, retirement, and disability are normal events in the life cycle and that productive adults are entitled to protection against the risks these life cycle events entail.

No society can survive without children. The rhetoric that holds children to be our greatest national resource is true, but the reality is that we do little to demonstrate any conviction of its truth. Becoming a parent and being a "good," concerned, and attentive parent may be the most significant contribution any adult can make to our society—and ultimately to the gross national product and to the future of the society. We acknowledge the contribution that elderly and retired workers have made. They benefit personally from that contribution, as does the society at large. Surely, it is time to acknowledge the contribution parents make in bearing, caring for, and rearing future generations of citizens, workers, and parents—even if they share personally in the rewards of having children. Surely, parenting is a life cycle stage warranting support at its inception and as an ongoing process by a society that needs and wants children. If we are convinced of this, we must, as a country, become more responsive to the needs of those large numbers of adults who now are trying to manage work and family responsibilities in an as yet unresponsive society.

Notes

1. See Sheila B. Kamerman and Alfred J. Kahn, *Child Care, Family Benefits and Working Parents: A Comparative Study* (New York: Columbia University Press, 1980); Alfred J. Kahn and Sheila B. Kamerman, *Social Services in International Perspective* (Washington, D.C.: U.S. Government Printing Office, 1977); Sheila B. Kamerman, "Work and Family in Industrialized Societies," *SIGNS: The Journal of Women in Culture and Society* (Summer 1979); and Sheila B. Kamerman and Alfred J. Kahn, "Comparative Analysis in Family Policy: A Case Study," *Social Work*, Vol. 24, No. 6 (November 1979).

2. A franc was worth, at this writing, about twenty-three cents.

3. The English terms "child-care center," "day nursery," "preschool," and "day care center" are used interchangeably to describe these programs in Sweden.

4. We should note that both the French and the West Germans are now experimenting with these "sibling" or "age-integrated" groups also.

5. Compulsory schooling does not begin in Sweden until age seven.

Appendix of Tables

TABLE A-1. Care Modes: A Consumer Survey

| | PERCENTAGES AND NUMBER OF CHILDREN IN CARE | | | |
| | Ages 0-2 Years | | Ages 3-5 Years | |
TYPE OF CARE	%	NO.	%	NO.*
In Own Home by Relative				
10–29 hours per week	3	245,900	3	302,100
30 + hours per week	3	239,900	2	178,200
In Own Home by Nonrelative				
20–29 hours per week	3	238,500	3	340,400
30 + hours per week	1	130,500	1	138,600
Relative's Home				
10–29 hours per week	4	402,500	4	471,300
30 + hours per week	3	287,300	3	346,700
Nonrelative's Home (Family Day Care)				
10–29 hours per week	3	286,000	3	302,800
30 + hours per week	4	364,600	4	394,100
Nursery and Day Care Center				
10–29 hours per week	2	106,300	5	493,800
30 + hours per week	2	179,700	6	708,700

Sources: *National Consumer Day Care Study*, Vol. II, Table VI (6–11); also, rate calculations from National Consumer Day Care Study as presented in Mary Jo Bane, "Child Care Arrangements of Working Parents," *Monthly Labor Review*, Vol. 102, No. 10 (October 1979). This table appears in Sheila B. Kamerman and Alfred J. Kahn, *Child Care, Family Benefits and Working Parents*.

*Note: These data do not include nursery school or other preschool attendance, and therefore are inaccurate for this age group, substantially understating the percentage of children of this age in care.

TABLE A–2. Child-Care Packages Per Preschool Child: The Component Parts

White, Two-Parent Families

	Pre-school	Family Day Care	Care in Relative's Home	Care by Spouse	In-Home Care by Other Relative	In-Home Care by Nonrelative[a]
Professional, managerial families $N = 28$ children (24 families)						
Two arrangements (N = 11)	8	3	2	5	—	4
Three arrangements (N = 7)	7	2	—	4	2	6
Four or more arrangements (N = 10)	10	6	5	9	2	10
Working-class families $N = 22$ children (18 families)						
Two arrangements (N = 9)	4	1	4	7	11	—
Three arrangements (N = 13)	8	4	6	10	5	4

Black, Two-Parent Families

Professional, managerial families
N = 19 children (16 families)

Two arrangements (N = 8)	7	4	2	2	—	1
Three arrangements (N = 7)	7	4	3	3	1	3
Four arrangements (N = 4)	3	4	3	3	—	3

Working-class families
N = 29 children (20 families)

Two arrangements (N = 17)	6	8	9	7	4	—
Three arrangements (N = 12)	8	7	7	6	7	1

TABLE A-2. (Cont.)

	Pre-school	Family Day Care	Care in Relative's Home	Care by Spouse	In-Home Care by Other Relative	In-Home Care by Nonrelative[a]
White, One-Parent Families						
N = 15 children (13 families)						
Two arrangements (N = 4)[b]	5	2	1	—	—	1
Three arrangements (N = 8)[b]	10	6	1	—	1	6
Four arrangements (N = 3)[b]	4	3	3	—	1	1
Black, One-Parent Families						
N = 16 children (14 families)						
Two arrangements (N = 14)	12	4	8	—	4	—
Three arrangements (N = 2)[b]	3	1	2	—	—	—

[a]In some cases this may mean a teenager, but in most instances the child-care person is an adult.
[b]One or more children attend both a day care center and a kindergarten program.

176

TABLE A-3. **Child-Care Arrangements for Working Mothers[a] By Race, Class, Family Structure, and Age of Child**

White, Professional/Managerial Families (N = 58)

Age	OUT-OF-HOME CARE ARRANGEMENTS[c]				IN-HOME CARE ARRANGEMENTS			Total Number of Children
	Day Care	Pre-school	Relative Care	Family Day Care (Nonrelative Care)	Father	Other Relative	Non-relative	
Two-parent[b]								
Under 3 years	1	½	2	5	2 2(½)	3	10 3(½)	26
3–5 years	2½	8 6(½)	½	2(½)	1 2(½)	1	3 6(½)	24 50
One-Parent								
Under 3 years	2	—	—	—	—	—	—	2
3–5 years	—	4½	½	1	—	—	—	6 8

TABLE A-3. (Cont.)

| Age | Out-of-Home Care Arrangements[c] | | | | In-Home Care Arrangements | | | Total Number of Children |
	Day Care	Pre-school	Relative Care	Family Day Care (Nonrelative Care)	Father	Other Relative	Non-relative	
	White, Clerical/Service/Blue-Collar Occupations, (N = 61)							
Two-Parent								
Under 3 years	1	2(½)	3(½)	1	12 5(½)	—	3	22
3–5 years	2	2 6(½)	1	—	3 3(½)	½	—	<u>13</u> 35[d]
One-Parent								
Under 3 years	2	—	1	3	—	—	1	7
3–5 years	11	5(½)	2 2(½)	2½	—	—	—	<u>19</u> 26

Black, Professional/Managerial Families (N = 40)

Two-Parent								
Under 3 years	3	(½)	4	7½	3	½	3½	22
3–5 years	4	8	—	—	—	—	—	<u>12</u>
								34[e]
One-Parent								
Under 3 years	1	1	—	1	—	—	—	3
3–5 years	—	2	—	1	—	—	—	<u>3</u>
								6

Black, Clerical/Service/Blue-Collar Occupations (N = 72)

Two-Parent								
Under 3 years	3	—	10	5	3	8	—	29
3–5 years	5	8	2	1	1	1	—	<u>18</u>
								47[f]

TABLE A–3. (Cont.)

Black, Clerical/Service/Blue Collar Occupations (N = 72)

	Out-of-Home Care Arrangements[c]				In-Home Care Arrangements			Total Number of Children
Age	Day Care	Pre-school	Relative Care	Family Day Care (Nonrelative Care)	Father	Other Relative	Non-relative	
One-Parent								
Under 3 years	2	—	6	4	1	—	—	13
3–5 years	10	—	—	—	—	2	—	<u>12</u>
								25[g]

[a] Almost all are working full time and none included here work less than thirty hours per week.
[b] There are forty-five mothers with fifty-two children in this subsample. One mother (with two children) was not employed and thus has been excluded from the table.
[c] This table accounts for only the dominant elements in a child's "care" package. We tabulate 3/4-day to full-day care as one. Anything between 1/2 and 3/4 = (½). Less than half-day is not counted.
[d] Thirty mothers, two who are family day care mothers and thus care for their own children while they work, are not included here; one other mother was not working full time and thus is not included here.
[e] Thirty mothers; one nonworking mother excluded from table.
[f] Thirty-eight mothers; one, who takes her child to work with her, is not included in the table.
[g] Twenty-six mothers; two, who leave their (2) children all week with a relative, are not included in the table.

T A B L E A-4.   Role of Women's Earnings in Family Economy

ROLE	NUMBER OF FAMILIES	PERCENTAGE OF FAMILIES
Sole Source of Income[a]	24	12
Major Source of Income[b]	81	40
Equal Contribution to Income	17	8
Contributes to Purchase of *Essentials* (e.g., rent, mortgage, food, medical bills)	64	31
Used for Personal Expenditures and Luxuries[c]	19	9
	205	100

[a]This does not include women who received supplementary income from public assistance or from child support. It includes single women whose earnings comprised total family income and six two-parent families in which the husbands were unemployed.

[b]Includes single women receiving public assistance or child support or where unemployed husband is receiving unemployment insurance benefits.

[c]Includes three women who were not working, but were seeking work.

Bibliography

ABT ASSOCIATES, INC. *National Day Care Study*. Washington, D.C.: Administration for Children, Youth, and Families of the Department of Health, Education, and Welfare, 1978–79.

ALONSO, WILLIAM. "Metropolis without Growth," *The Public Interest*, No. 53, Fall 1978.

BANE, MARY JO. *Here to Stay: American Families in the Twentieth Century*. New York: Basic Books, 1976.

BANE, MARY JO, et al. "Child Care Arrangements of Working Parents," *Monthly Labor Review*, Vol. 102, No. 10, October 1979.

BARRETT, NANCY. "The Family in Transition." Washington, D.C.: The Urban Institute, 1978. Processed.

BEDNARZIK, ROBERT W. and Deborah P. Klein. "Labor Force Trends: A Synthesis and Analysis," *Monthly Labor Review*, October 1977.

BRONFENBRENNER, URIE. "The Origins of Alienation," *Scientific American*, Vol. 231, 1974.

BRONFENBRENNER, URIE. *The Ecology of Human Development*. Cambridge, Mass.: Harvard University Press, 1979.

CAHN, ANN FOOTE, ed. *American Workers in a Full Employment Economy*. Washington, D.C.: Government Printing Office, 1977.

FEINSTEIN, KAREN WOLK, ed. *Working Women and Families*. Beverly Hills, Calif.: Sage Publications, 1979.

FRIEDEN, BERNARD J. "The New Housing Cost Problem," *The Public Interest*, No. 53, Fall 1978.

GLICK, PAUL C., and ARTHUR NORTON. "Marrying, Divorcing and Living Together in the U.S. Today," *Population Bulletin* (Washington, D.C.: Population Reference Bureau, Inc.), Vol. 32, No. 5, October 1977.

HAREVEN, TAMARA K. "Modernization and Family History: Perspectives on Social Change," *SIGNS: The Journal of Women in Culture and Society*, Vol. 2, No. 1, Autumn 1976.

HAYGHE, HOWARD. "Marital and Family Characteristics of Workers, March, 1977," *Monthly Labor Review*, February 1978.

HAYGHE, HOWARD. "Working Wives' Contributions to Family Incomes in 1977," *Monthly Labor Review*, Vol. 102, No. 10, October 1979.

JOHNSON, BEVERLY L. "Women Who Head Families, 1970–1977: Their Numbers Rose, Income Lagged," *Monthly Labor Review*, February 1978.

JOHNSON, BEVERLY L., and HOWARD HAYGHE. "Labor Force Participation of Married Women, March, 1976," *Monthly Labor Review*, Vol. 100, No. 6, June 1977.

KAHN, ALFRED J., and SHEILA B. KAMERMAN. *Social Services in International Perspective*. Washington, D.C.: Government Printing Office, 1977.

KAMERMAN, SHEILA B. "Work and Family Life in Industrialized Societies," *SIGNS: The Journal of Women in Culture and Society*, Summer 1979.

KAMERMAN, SHEILA B., and ALFRED J. KAHN. "European Family Policy Currents: The Question of Families with Very Young Children," in U.S. Senate, Subcommittee on Child and Human Development of the Committee on Human Resources, and House of Representatives, Subcommittee on Select Education of the Committee on Education and Labor, Report of Hearings, *White House Conference on Families, 1978*. Washington, D.C.: Government Printing Office, 1978.

KAMERMAN, SHEILA B., and ALFRED J. KAHN, eds. *Family Policy: Government and Families in Fourteen Countries*. New York: Columbia University Press, 1978.

KAMERMAN, SHEILA B., and ALFRED J. KAHN. "Comparative Analysis in Family Policy: A Case Study," *Social Work*, Vol. 24, No. 6, November 1979.

KAMERMAN, SHEILA B., and ALFRED J. KAHN. "Day Care: A Wider View," *The Public Interest*, Winter 1979.

KAMERMAN, SHEILA B., and ALFRED J. KAHN. *Child Care, Family Benefits and Working Parents*. New York: Columbia University Press, 1980.

KANTER, ROSABETH MOSS. *Work and Family in the United States: A Critical Review and Agenda for Research and Policy*. New York: Russell Sage Foundation, 1977.

KENISTON, KENNETH. *All Our Children*. New York: Harcourt Brace Jovanovich, 1977.

KREPS, JUANITA M., ed. *Women and the American Economy*. Englewood Cliffs, N.J.: Prentice-Hall, 1976.

LEIN, LAURA, et al. *Work and Family Life*. Cambridge, Mass.: Center for the Study of Public Policy, 1974. Preliminary report, processed.

MEYER, MITCHELL. *Women and Employee Benefits*. New York: The Conference Board, 1978.

MORONEY, ROBERT. *The Family and the State*. New York: Longmans, 1976.

MYRDAL, ALVA, and VIOLA KLEIN. *Women's Two Roles*. London: Routledge and Kegan Paul, 1962.

NEILSEN, A. C., COMPANY. *Wage-Earning Mothers: A National Profile*. September 1978.

NEW YORK MINORITY TASK FORCE ON CHILD CARE. *Day Care: How We Care in New York State*. Albany: New York State Senate, Legislative Document, 1978, No. SO 3216.

PLECK, JOSEPH H., et al. *Work and Family Life*, Draft report, September 1978. Wellesley, Mass.: Wellesley College Center for Research on Women, 1978.

RAPOPORT, ROBERT, and RHONA RAPOPORT. *Dual Career Families*. London: Penguin, 1971.

RAPOPORT, ROBERT, and RHONA RAPOPORT. "Men, Women and Equity," *The Family Coordinator*, Vol. 24, No. 4, 1975.

RAPOPORT, ROBERT, and RHONA RAPOPORT. *Dual Career Families Re-Examined*. New York: Harper & Row, 1977.

RAPOPORT, ROBERT, and RHONA RAPOPORT. "Dual Career Families: Progress and Prospects," *Marriage and Family Review*, Vol. 1, No. 5, September/October 1978.

RAPOPORT, ROBERT, and RHONA RAPOPORT, eds. *Working Couples*. New York: Harper Colophon, 1978.

ROSS, HEATHER L., and ISABEL V. SAWHILL. *Time of Transition: The Growth of Families Headed by Women*. Washington, D.C.: The Urban Institute, 1975.

SMITH, RALPH E., ed. *The Subtle Revolution: Women at Work*. Washington, D.C.: The Urban Institute, 1979.

UNCO, *National Child Care Consumer Study: 1975*. Washington, D.C.: Department of Health, Education, and Welfare, 1976.

U.S., BUREAU OF THE CENSUS. *Current Population Reports*, Series P-20, No. 318, "Nursery School and Kindergarten Enrollment of Children and Labor Force Status of Their Mothers: October, 1967–October, 1976." Washington, D.C.: Government Printing Office, 1978.

U.S., BUREAU OF THE CENSUS. *Current Population Reports*, Series P-20, No. 319, "School Enrollment—Social and Economic Characteristics of Students: October, 1976." Washington, D.C.: Government Printing Office, 1978.

U.S., BUREAU OF THE CENSUS. *Current Population Reports*, Series P-20, No. 324, "Population Profile of the United States: 1977." Washington, D.C.: Government Printing Office, 1978.

U.S., BUREAU OF THE CENSUS. *Current Population Reports*, Series P-60, No. 114, "Money Income in 1976 of Families and Persons in the United States." Washington, D.C.: Government Printing Office, 1978.

U.S., BUREAU OF THE CENSUS. *Current Population Reports*, Series P-60, No. 115, "Characteristics of the Population Below the Poverty Level: 1976." Washington, D.C.: Government Printing Office, 1978.

U.S., CONGRESSIONAL BUDGET OFFICE. *Child Care and Preschool: Options for Federal Support*. Washington, D.C.: Government Printing Office, 1978.

U.S., DEPARTMENT OF LABOR, BUREAU of LABOR STATISTICS. *U.S. Working Women: A Data Book, 1977*. Washington, D.C.: Government Printing Office, 1977.

U.S., HOUSE OF REPRESENTATIVES, SELECT COMMITTEE ON POPULATION. *Hearings, May–June, 1978*. Washington, D.C.: Government Printing Office, 1978.

U.S., HOUSE OF REPRESENTATIVES, SELECT COMMITTEE ON POPULATION. *Domestic Consequences of United States Population Change*. Washington, D.C.: Government Printing Office, December 1978.

U.S., SENATE, SUBCOMMITTEE ON LABOR OF THE COMMITTEE ON HUMAN RESOURCES. Report of Hearings, April 1977, *Discrimination on the Basis of Pregnancy, 1977*. Washington, D.C.: Government Printing Office, 1977.

U.S. LEAGUE OF SAVINGS ASSOCIATIONS. *Homeownership: Affording the Single Family Home*. Washington, D.C., 1977.

VICKERY, CLAIRE. "Economics and the Single Mother Family," *Public Welfare*, Vol. 36, No. 1, Winter 1978.

VICKERY, CLAIRE. "The Changing Household: Implications for Devising an Income Support Program," *Public Policy*, Vol. XXVI, No. 1, Winter 1978.

WALDMAN, ELIZABETH, et al. "Working Mothers in the 1970s: A Look at the Statistics," *Monthly Labor Review*, Vol. 102, No. 10, October 1979.

Index